Working with the revised Early Years Foundation Stage

Principles into Practice

JULIAN GRENIER

WITH THANKS TO:

Many people helped with the drafting of this document. They're not responsible for any of the content, opinions or errors below, but they are thanked for their generosity.

Everyone on the team at Sheringham Nursery School and Children's Centre.

Everyone in the Newham Early Years Hub and East London Early Years and Schools Partnership.

The 200 practitioners who shaped the final version of this document with feedback and suggestions.

The researchers and academics who gave their time to reviewing and improving this document including Professors Iram Siraj, Kathy Sylva, Ted Melhuish, Lynn Ang, Kevan Collins and Alison Peacock; Doctors Amelia Roberts, Sara Bonetti, Peter Elfer, Sinéad Harmey, Lala Manners and Sandra Mathers.

The team at TeachFirst including Viki Dobbs and Victoria Blake.

The team at PACEY including Liz Bayram and Penny Tassoni.

The team at Harris Federation including Matt Britt and Laura Bairstow.

Amy Clark, Ben Smith, Bernadette Duffy, Cassie Buchanan, Deena Billings, Denise Morrisroe, Ed Vainker, Isabel Davis, Jan Dubiel, Jean Gross, Lesley Curtis, Louisa Reeves, Lydia Cuddy-Gibbs, Mary Hartshorne, Megan Dixon, Megan Pacey, Michael Freeston, Sarah Tillotson and Stella Ziolkowski.

CONTENTS

ACKNOWLEDGMENTS

Illustrations: Juli Dosad Design Studio © 2020

Photographs: Jonathan Smith, Grasmere School and Nursery, Cumbria, Justin Thomas Photography and iStock.com

.

THE IMPORTANCE OF EARLY CHILDHOOD EDUCATION AND CARE

Most children have their first experience away from their immediate family and family friends when they come to an early years setting. Early Years settings are at the heart of their local communities. They provide safe and nurturing spaces for children to play and learn together. Together, children learn about respecting other people, co-operating and sharing. They learn about being true to themselves and respecting the rights of others.

The United Nations Convention on the Rights of the Child states that children have a right to education without discrimination. Education should ensure children respect and understand the rights of others.

These ideas underpin democracy and the values of modern British society.

The Statutory Framework for the Early Years Foundation Stage (Early Adopter version, 2020) states that four guiding principles should shape practice in early years settings. These are:

- every child is a unique child, who is constantly learning and can be resilient, capable, confident and self-assured

- children learn to be strong and independent through positive relationships

1

- children learn and develop well in enabling environments with teaching and support from adults, who respond to their individual interests and needs and help them to build their learning over time. Children benefit from a strong partnership between practitioners and parents and/or carers. (See "the characteristics of effective teaching and learning" at paragraph 1.15)

- children develop and learn at different rates. The framework covers the education and care of all children in early years provision, including children with special educational needs and disabilities.

The EYFS is a distinct and important phase in education. It places an equal priority on supporting children's social and emotional development, and their learning. The early years are the crucial time for developing children's enjoyment of learning, their engagement and motivation. It's an important time for children develop their ability to persist and show gritty determination.

The practitioners who work in the early years guide and shape young children. They create a sense of friendly co-operation. They also set clear rules and limits. This shows that they value each child as an individual, and help each child to live and learn alongside others. They play and have conversations with children. This is how practitioners help children to manage and enjoy being a group, share and take turns. In the early years, children learn new vocabulary and knowledge across different areas of learning. They learn to decide what they want to do, and how to solve different problems along the way. These experiences help them to develop skills which will benefit them throughout their education, and the rest of their lives.

Parents are essential partners in children's early learning. Both the home and the early years setting can each do a great deal to support the child. They achieve even more when they work co-operatively together in a respectful partnership.

There is no single blueprint for the early years curriculum – in other words, what we want children to learn. Nor is there a single approach to pedagogy – helping children to learn. It's up to settings and childminders to make these decisions.

This document seeks to explain much of thinking behind *Development Matters*. It summarises the underpinning knowledge and research evidence which can help practitioners in their work. Leaders and managers can use the Seven key features of effective practice to structure initial training and ongoing professional development for practitioners and teams.

This guidance is intended to support children as they grow up happy, healthy, curious and ready for the next stage of their education.

Throughout this document, 'early years setting' is used to mean childminders, private, voluntary and community nurseries and daycare facilities, nursery and reception classes in schools, and maintained nursery schools.

'Parent' is used to mean parents, carers and guardians.

To simplify the design of this publication, full references have not been given for online publications. The free PDF of this book includes hyperlinks which you can click on for quick and easy access to all of the online references.

Seven Features of Effective Practice

1 The best for every child

- All children deserve to have an equal chance of success.

- High-quality early education is good for all children. It is especially important for children from disadvantaged backgrounds.

- When they start school, children from disadvantaged backgrounds are, on average, 4 months behind their peers. We need to do more to narrow that gap.

- Children who have lived through difficult experiences can begin to grow stronger when they experience high quality early education and care.

- High-quality early education and care is inclusive. Children's special educational needs and disabilities (SEND) are identified quickly. All children promptly receive any extra help they need, so they can progress well in their learning.

2 High-quality care

- The child's experience must always be central to the thinking of every practitioner.

- Babies, toddlers and young children thrive when they are loved and well cared for.

- High-quality care is consistent. Every practitioner needs to enjoy spending time with young children.

- Effective practitioners are responsive to children and babies. They notice when a baby looks towards them and gurgles and respond with pleasure.

- Practitioners understand that toddlers are learning to be independent, so they will sometimes get frustrated.

- Practitioners know that starting school, and all the other transitions in the early years, are big steps for small children.

3 The curriculum: what we want children to learn

- The curriculum is a top-level plan of everything the early years setting wants the children to learn.

- Planning to help every child to develop their language is vital.

- The curriculum needs to be ambitious. Careful sequencing will help children to build their learning over time.

- Young children's learning is often driven by their interests. Plans need to be flexible.

- Babies and young children do not develop in a fixed way. Their development is like a spider's web with many strands, not a straight line.

- Depth in early learning is much more important than covering lots of things in a superficial way.

4 Pedagogy: helping children to learn

• Children are powerful learners. Every child can make progress in their learning, with the right help.

• Effective pedagogy is a mix of different approaches. Children learn through play, by adults modelling, by observing each other, and through guided learning and direct teaching.

• Practitioners carefully organise enabling environments for high-quality play. Sometimes, they make time and space available for children to invent their own play. Sometimes, they join in to sensitively support and extend children's learning.

• Children in the early years also learn through group work, when practitioners guide their learning.

• Older children need more of this guided learning.

• A well-planned learning environment, indoors and outside, is an important aspect of pedagogy.

5 Assessment: checking what children have learnt

• Assessment is about noticing what children can do and what they know. It is not about lots of data and evidence.

• Effective assessment requires practitioners to understand child development. Practitioners also need to be clear about what they want children to know and be able to do.

• Accurate assessment can highlight whether a child has a special educational need and needs extra help.

• Before assessing children, it's a good idea to think about whether the assessments will be useful.

• Assessment should not take practitioners away from the children for long periods of time.

6 Self-regulation and executive function

• Executive function includes the child's ability to:
  • hold information in mind
  • focus their attention
  • regulate their behaviour
  • plan what to do next.

• These abilities contribute to the child's growing ability to self-regulate:
  • focus their thinking
  • monitor what they are doing and adapt
  • regulate strong feelings
  • be patient for what they want
  • bounce back when things get difficult.

• Language development is central to self-regulation: children use language to guide their actions and plans. Pretend play gives many opportunities for children to focus their thinking, persist and plan ahead.

7 Partnership with parents

• It is important for parents and early years settings to have a strong and respectful partnership. This sets the scene for children to thrive in the early years.

• This includes listening regularly to parents and giving parents clear information about their children's progress.

• The help that parents give their children at home has a very significant impact on their learning.

• Some children get much less support for their learning at home than others. By knowing and understanding all the children and their families, settings can offer extra help to those who need it most.

• It is important to encourage all parents to chat, play and read with their children.

IMPROVING QUALITY

Quality matters to all children. But it matters especially for disadvantaged children. So, it's important for every early years setting to have a plan to improve quality and to support any children who might be in danger of falling behind the majority.

Effective early years settings are always ambitious to become better.

Professional Development can lead to improvements in quality. But, in practice, it doesn't always succeed in that. Professional Development has to be planned carefully, delivered well and regularly evaluated. It needs to be seen as a year-round activity, not a one-off event.

It's important to start with a clear understanding of your local context: what do children bring to your setting? What do they need you to offer them? What does your assessment information tell you about the progress children make? All of this information can help you to pinpoint priorities for improvement. You might need to focus more on certain areas of the curriculum: for example, if many of your children have limited space to play, you might need to spend more time on supporting their physical development.

Once your aims are clear, you are ready to plan your Professional Development programme. This is most likely to be effective if it's based on the best available evidence and clearly focused on improving children's experiences in your setting. Consider how your programme will lead to:

- children learning better
- children having improved health and wellbeing
- children experiencing better care.

You can look for evidence of what works in the Early Intervention Foundation's 2018 report, *Teaching, pedagogy and practice in early years childcare: An evidence review* or on the Education Endowment Foundation's online Early Years Toolkit. The evidence suggests that a successful programme will run over a whole year, or the majority of the year. Each practitioner will engage in at least 20 hours of training in total. Those 20 hours might

6

include a whole-staff session, self-study and online learning, discussion, mentoring or coaching, and peer support. There isn't any evidence that sending staff to one-off training events and asking them to share their learning with the wider team is effective in improving quality, although it might support an individual's professional development.

Professional development is most effective when there is a clear focus on practice, clearly linked to theory. Ongoing support will mean that participants can transfer what they are learning into their daily practice, and understand the theory that underpins what they are doing. For example, practitioners could regularly observe or film their practice (with the consent of parents). That will help them to check that they are putting their training into action. Coaching sessions can help practitioners to keep focused on their training, and to overcome barriers to change.

It's important to include everyone in the training and implementation sessions. Ensure that sessions are engaging and practical, with focused professional learning and plenty of practical examples. Participants will need to know what the new practice looks like. Settings can reduce the costs of Professional Development by joining together as a group and working together on a programme. Local authorities, Teaching School Hubs, and Research Schools can help with this.

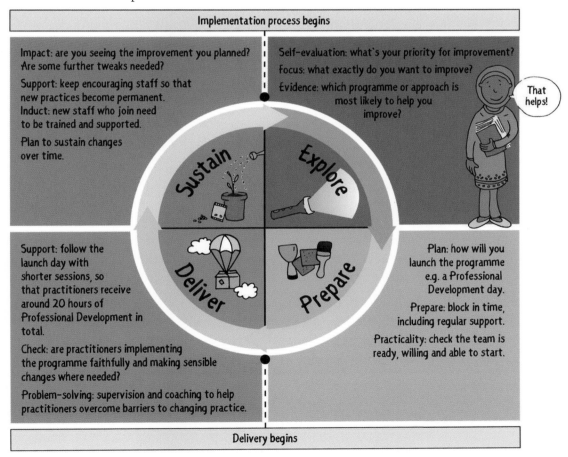

Figure 1: Implementing change

(adapted from *Putting Evidence to Work,* Education Endowment Foundation, 2019)

Effective professional development gives practitioners a secure grounding in:

Content	<ul><li>how children develop and learn</li><li>what children need to learn (content)</li><li>how to help children's learning (pedagogy)</li></ul>
Interactions with children	<ul><li>how to support children's emotional wellbeing</li><li>how to listen to children, have conversations with them, and build their language and vocabulary</li><li>how to encourage children's early learning. This includes supportive, thoughtful and gently challenging interactions</li><li>how to respond appropriately to children's individual, cultural and developmental needs</li></ul>

Adult learning

Practitioners need time to discuss and reflect on their learning. They must have opportunities to try out new ways of working. They also need to receive feedback on how they are doing, and how they can keep improving their practice.

Leadership and management

An effective programme of professional development is carefully planned. It takes account of the context and performance of the setting. The content of the professional development is chosen with care, drawing on robust research and evidence.

One-off workshops, after-work sessions ('twilights') and days are not likely to be effective. Practitioners benefit from sustained programmes of professional development which are regularly reviewed throughout the year. Then the team can check which aspects of improving practice are working and which need further support. Some changes might not be working, so they can be stopped.

Peer feedback, regular support, videoing and reflecting on your own practice, mentoring and coaching can be effective. The focus needs to be helping practitioners to put their learning into practice.

Effective professional development improves the quality of interactions between children and practitioners. It supports the development and implementation of a high-quality curriculum.

Individual settings and childminders know their children, families and local communities. They understand both the strengths which children bring in every day, and the challenges they may face. They can use this knowledge to set out and implement their curriculum.

Development Matters and the Early Learning Goals are not curriculum plans.

	Key questions: what is a high-quality curriculum?
The big picture	• What are the overall aims, values and approach of the setting or school? • How will the curriculum be suitable for the children, their families, and the local community? • How will the curriculum be ambitious for every child?
Content	• What do we want the children to learn? • Is this consistent with the educational programmes set out in the EYFS Statutory Framework?
Approach	• How will we help all children to learn (pedagogy)? • How will we ensure all children are healthy and developing personally, socially and emotionally? • What routines will provide the right type of care, reassurance and atmosphere for learning? • How will we arrange resources and manage the learning environment to ensure that all children can access and benefit from what we offer? • How will we make best use of the Early Years Pupil Premium to support the learning of disadvantaged children? • How will we make sure any plans we make are flexible and open to individual children's interests? Will we be able to make the most of unexpected opportunities which may arise?
Assessment	• How will we check that children are learning what we want them to? • How will we make sure we notice learning that we were not necessarily expecting? • How will we prioritise assessment in the here-and-now (formative assessment)? • How will we make sure we act quickly on formative assessment, to help children's learning?

Assessment (cont.)	• How will we manage assessment at key points (summative assessment)? This includes two statutory assessments. They are the 2-year development check and the Early Years Foundation Stage Profile.
	• How will we ensure that assessment procedures don't take practitioners away from the children for extended periods of time? How will we avoid unnecessary workload?
Evaluation	• How will you check that the curriculum is working, and prioritise what needs improvement?
	• How will we check that the curriculum is effective in preparing children for the next phase of their learning?
	• How will we gather and consider feedback from children, practitioners, parents and others?

Where children are not experiencing success, they may have barriers to their learning. These barriers might be short-term, or they might indicate a longer-term special educational need and/or disability. In these instances, more assessment will be needed to try to get to know the child better, and pinpoint their needs. In turn, this helps practitioners to work with parents and plan for any appropriate extra help. This might involve further support in the setting. Some children need specialist equipment. Some children benefit from targeted interventions which have been planned by a specialist.

Accurate assessment which is acted on quickly can help to maximise every child's learning and respond quickly to their interests. But, assessment does not need to dominate early years practice. Writing observations and taking photographs cannot, in themselves, help children's learning. Practitioner workload associated with collecting data and tracking should be kept to a minimum. Settings need to assess and monitor children's progress only insofar as this helps them to do the best for every child.

Quality matters for all children, especially those who are in danger of falling behind the majority. When children have a positive experience of early education and care, it can change their lives for the better. It can help children overcome early disadvantage. It can help children overcome developmental difficulties which may have resulted from less stimulating earlier experiences. It can reduce the incidence of special educational needs.

Research, like the EPPSE Project, demonstrates that these positive effects last all the way through children's primary and secondary schooling.

This guidance is not intended to box in practitioners. The statements in *Development Matters* are not intended as a series of hoops that every child must jump through at particular times. Broader, professional decisions about what's best for the children drive effective practice in settings and schools.

Curriculum Guidance for the Early Years Foundation Stage draws on robust research and examples of best practice. It can help practitioners ensure that children are well prepared for the next steps in their learning.

●	Iram Siraj and others (2018) *Fostering Effective Early Learning (FEEL) Study*
●	Sue Rogers and others (2020) *A systematic review of the evidence-base for professional learning in early years education (THE PLEYE REVIEW)*
●	Sandra Mathers (2019) *Training: the right mix* (Nursery World Management, Spring 2019)
●	Taggart, B., Sylva, K., Melhuish, E., Sammons, P. and Siraj, I. (2015) *Effective pre-school, primary and secondary education project (EPPSE 3-16+)*

Find out more

- Iram Siraj and others (2018) *Fostering Effective Early Learning (FEEL) Study*

- Sue Rogers and others (2020) *A systematic review of the evidence-base for professional learning in early years education (THE PLEYE REVIEW)*

- Sandra Mathers (2019) *Training: the right mix* (Nursery World Management, Spring 2019)

- Taggart, B., Sylva, K., Melhuish, E., Sammons, P. and Siraj, I. (2015) *Effective pre-school, primary and secondary education project (EPPSE 3-16+)*

THE BEST FOR EVERY CHILD

- All children deserve to have an equal chance of success.

- High-quality early education is good for all children. It is especially important for children from disadvantaged backgrounds.

- When they start school, children from disadvantaged backgrounds are, on average, 4 months behind their peers. We need to do more to narrow that gap.

- Children who have lived through difficult experiences can begin to grow stronger when they experience high-quality early education and care.

- High-quality early education and care is inclusive. Children's special educational needs and disabilities (SEND) are identified quickly. All children promptly receive any extra help they need, so they can progress well in their learning.

Inequality can damage children's health, development and learning from an early age. However, high-quality early education and childcare can play a part in tackling this problem.

High-quality early education and childcare can help to break the 'cycle of disadvantage', which can otherwise lead to poor children growing up to become poor adults without the qualifications and skills they need to get on in life.

Every child and family is unique. It's important not to make negative assumptions about disadvantaged children. Instead of making assumptions, we need to know, value and understand the children we are working with.

Many families in disadvantaged circumstances do a great job supporting their children's learning.

However, it's important to note that on average, by the time they are 5 years old, disadvantaged children are already behind in their development. The gap is particularly wide in language. At age five, there is a seventeen month gap between the vocabulary of the most and least disadvantaged children.

The Education Endowment Foundation comments:

The attainment gap

'The gap begins in the early years and is already evident when children begin school aged 5.

'The gap grows wider at every following stage of education: it more than doubles to 9.5 months by the end of primary school, and then more than doubles again, to 19.3 months, by the end of secondary school. This shows the importance of intervening early and then of continuing to attend to the needs of disadvantaged pupils.'

The Attainment Gap (Education Endowment Foundation, 2017, p. 2)

The early years play a crucial role in making life-chances more equal for everyone. Every child can make progress, with the right support.

There are also many other factors which can have a negative impact on a child's health and development. These are 'risk factors': there are no simple predictors of a child's future outcomes.

Risk factors include:

- unemployment, low income and job stress

- conflict between parents

- parents experiencing mental health difficulties

- poor and overcrowded housing

- experiencing or witnessing violence in the local community

- being discriminated against (for example, being subject to racism).

These risk factors make it harder for families to provide well for children's early learning. If there is little opportunity for a young child to play, talk and enjoy books and other educational materials at home, then their development will be adversely affected.

Adverse Childhood Experiences (ACEs) are potentially traumatic events that occur in childhood, like being abused as a child. This includes the emotional abuse from witnessing violence between parents.

The Marmot Review: Ten Years On comments that:

Adverse childhood experiences

'Children growing up in deprived areas, in poverty, and those of a lower socioeconomic position are more likely to be exposed to ACEs compared with their more advantaged peers. ACEs elevate the risk that children and young people will experience damage to health, or to other social outcomes, across the life course. ACEs have long-term and negative effects.'

Health Equity in England: The Marmot Report 10 years on (The Institute of Health Equity, 2020, p. 45)

High-quality early education and childcare plays a positive role by helping children to become more resilient. A child's resilience is the extent to which they can overcome earlier, negative experiences. A key factor which helps children to overcome adversity is having at least one warm, positive and nurturing relationship. In an early years setting, a strong relationship with a key person, extending to wider relationships with other adults and with children, can help children to become stronger and more resilient over time.

Equality and Diversity

The Statutory Framework for the Early Years Foundation Stage promotes equality and non-discrimination. In particular, the Equality Act 2010 requires early years providers to protect people from discrimination on the basis of 9 'protected characteristics'. These are:

- age
- disability
- gender reassignment
- marriage and civil partnership
- pregnancy and maternity
- race
- religion or belief
- sex
- sexual orientation.

Section 149 of the Equality Act 2010 includes the Public Sector Equality Duty (PSED). This requires early years providers in receipt of government funding to have due regard to the need to:

- Eliminate unlawful discrimination, harassment and victimisation and other conduct prohibited by the Equality Act 2010

- Advance equality of opportunity between people who share a protected characteristic and those who do not

- Foster good relations between people who share a protected characteristic and those who do not.

The Equality Act protections are relevant to the workforce and to the children in early years provision together with their families.

Leaders, managers and practitioners are required to show due regard to the need to promote equality and eliminate discrimination when setting the curriculum. This should include consideration of:

- the learning environment and resources

- the minute-by-minute interactions with children

- the setting's partnership with parents.

Examples of actions which early years providers can take, include:

- Encouraging children from different backgrounds to share activities

- Combatting stereotypical views of what boys and girls can do

- Promoting respect for ethnic and linguistic diversity: this includes supporting parents and children to use their first language at home and in the setting, where that first language is not English

- Combating stereotypical views about people from different ethnic, religious and cultural backgrounds.

Early education and childcare will only benefit disadvantaged children if there is a strong focus on quality. The Education Policy Institute notes the two main dimensions of quality:

Quality in childcare and early education

- *structural quality*: the 'iron triangle': workforce training and professional development, child-to-staff ratios and group size

- *process quality*: the practices which lead to 'favourable outcomes for children across the domains of language and literacy, mathematics, cognitive, socio-emotional and physical outcomes.'

Education Policy Institute, 2018

High-quality settings understand the different needs and experiences of individual children, their families, and their communities. They celebrate cultural and linguistic diversity. They appropriately manage any specific issues that arise, so that every child benefits from their early education. As a result, they help children to develop the knowledge, attitudes, skills and fluency in English they need as they grow up in 21st century England.

Unconscious bias

Within these broader questions of equality, each practitioner will need to reflect on the role of unconscious bias. Everyone, at some time, will draw on stereotypes to make sense of the world around them. It is common to see young boys as wanting to be outdoors, active and boisterous, whereas young girls may be praised for being 'good' and helpful.

In wider society, stereotypes affect many groups of children. For example, African-Caribbean children are commonly seen as particularly gifted in their musical abilities and physical skills. As children become aware of the stereotypes associated with their group, they may become anxious. This can affect their development and learning. Girls might feel that they are no good at climbing trees, and might not even try to develop their confidence and skills. Boys might feel that the book area and drawing table are not places for them.

Unconscious bias affects everyone. It affects the way we play and talk with children. So, it is important to have time to reflect, to stand back and look at what different children are learning and how we are relating to them. Are all the girls clustered around female practitioners, talking and being sociable? Are the boys far away from the practitioners, and missing out on these opportunities? Are children from some ethnic groups less involved in activities? Promoting equality means giving every child access to the provision. It means giving every child the teaching they need to develop well across all the areas of the Early Years Foundation Stage. Sometimes it will mean taking steps to remove barriers faced by particular children.

Likewise, it is important for practitioners to be interested in the children and families they work with, and to feel confident to ask them questions in a respectful way. That builds understanding of how every family is unique. It also helps practitioners to understand the aspects of a culture or religion that the family shares with others. When questions are 'shut down', learning is shut down too. Staff, children and parents will benefit from understanding the differences and identifying the similarities we all share. Instead of feeling stressed about

16

saying the wrong thing, or showing bias, it can be better to become aware of our biases and work to overcome them.

Everyone has a leadership role in an early years team to promote and champion equality. A focus on diversity can help each person to feel that they have particular qualities to bring to the staff team. It can help each child to feel unique and special. Then children, families and staff can feel more confident about 'being themselves'. They can feel safe in the knowledge that any inappropriate language, bias or behaviour will be challenged.

Supporting Children with Special Educational Needs and/or Disabilities (SEND)

Under the Equality Act (2010), Early Years providers have a duty to make reasonable adjustments for disabled children. The aim of making adjustments is, as far as possible, to remove any disadvantage faced by disabled children.

In recent years, outcomes for children by the end of the EYFS have improved. But they have not improved as much for children with SEND. Disabled children, and children with special educational needs, make less progress than non-disabled children. That's the case even when they have similar levels of cognitive skills (similar levels of development on entry).

So, it is important to spend time observing and assessing children who don't seem to be progressing as well as you might expect them to. Sometimes, getting to know the child better will help them through a difficult phase in their development. Many children have 'ups and downs'. At those times, they may need extra help and attention.

But there will be other children who, despite your best efforts, continue to experience difficulties. Those difficulties could be in the areas of communication, physical development or their emotional wellbeing and behaviour. Practitioners must discuss such concerns with children's parents and agree how they will work together. It is often important to bring colleagues from health into this discussion, for example the child's health visitor.

Joined-up assessment involving health, Early Years and other agencies can have a powerful and positive impact on children. When health and Early Years practitioners work closely with parents to check children's development at two, early difficulties can be detected. Then everyone can work together to support the child.

Many young children may have an unmet health need. The Education Endowment Foundation notes that:

Undiagnosed health needs

'It is possible that around 13% of children in the U.K. may have an undiagnosed need. These issues can affect all children, but those from disadvantaged backgrounds and certain ethnicities are more likely to be affected.'

Preparing for Literacy: Improving Communication, Language and Literacy in the Early Years

(Education Endowment Foundation, 2018, p. 21)

Is it important for every child to eat well and be physically active. The United Kingdoms' Chief Medical Officers advise that young children should be active for 180 minutes per day:

Figure 2: Physical activity guidelines: infographics (2019)

It's important for early years settings to focus both on helping children to be healthy, and helping them to be successful learners. They are connected together. Children who are successful learners and communicators grow up to be healthier adults. 'Strong communication and language skills in the early years are linked with success in education, higher levels of qualifications, higher wages and better health' (The Institute of Health Equity, 2020, p. 38).

Careful and precise observation of a child who appears to be struggling in one or more aspects of their development is essential. It can help practitioners to identify what the barriers to their learning appear to be.

On the other hand, it isn't helpful to keep using the same strategies when they are not working. It may be important to consider whether different approaches might meet the child's needs better.

For example, imagine a 3-year-old starting nursery. She seems to be unable to interact and play with the other children. Just continuing to 'offer' her play opportunities may not help her. There is a barrier to her learning. She can't interact with other children. A Speech and Language Therapist might suggest a new strategy to help her. A visual timetable with symbols for some of the different activities might help her plan what she would like to do. It might encourage her to choose what to take part in. The other children in the provision need to learn how to communicate using those symbols. Then they will be able to interact with her, too, and include her in their play.

The right to high-quality early education and care

Every child has the right to high-quality early education and care. That means more than just offering 'the same to everyone'. Practitioners need to consider the individual support and specific resources that a particular child might need. Then, that child can begin to achieve their full potential.

Practitioners must consider if a child has a special educational need or disability which requires specialist support. Then, they can help families to access, relevant services from other agencies as appropriate for additional support in the setting, and at home. In addition, settings can also seek advice from the local authority's Area SENCOs. They provide advice and guidance to early years providers on the development of inclusive early learning environments. The Area SENCO helps make the links between education, health and social care to help ensure that children with SEN have appropriate early provision. They also support with the transition to compulsory schooling.

There are four areas of special educational need which practitioners need to consider:

- cognition and learning

- communication and interaction

- social, emotional and mental health

- physical and sensory needs.

All children are entitled to take part in play and learning in an Early Years setting. That means thinking carefully about curriculum planning, routines, resources and the organisation of the learning environment. For example, all children need activities which help them to learn language and new vocabulary. This learning can be incidental, when they are choosing their own play. Or they can learn new language and vocabulary in carefully planned discrete teaching sessions. Either way, children who have difficulties with their communication and interaction will especially benefit.

Disabled children may need adaptations to be made, so that they can access all of the resources and learning on offer. Often the child's disability results more from social barriers than their personal impairment. For example, a child using a walking frame needs more space between furniture to be able to get into areas like the home corner. A child with an autism spectrum disorder may need visual signs in every part of the provision. All the adults and the children will need to know how to communicate with these signs so that child can be included in their play and learning. Every adaptation is a positive step to help every child receive a high standard of Early Years education and care.

Children are curious and they will have plenty of questions to ask about other children who look or act differently to them. It's important to be positive about this and to answer questions with honesty. Be clear and use respectful language. For example, a new child may look different to other children because of scarring. Or part of their face or body might work differently to other children's. Practitioners will need to reassure the child that they value and accept them. It will be helpful to allow other children to ask questions, and respond clearly to them: for example, *Leila's face might look different, but she is just the same as anyone else*. It's important to check with children's parents first about how they would like questions like these to be answered.

So, to meet the needs of children with SEND, a setting must have the foundations of high-quality practice securely in place for every child. For those children who are not making sound progress, targeted interventions might help. The child who is not taking part in any messy play may have sensory needs. They may need to be introduced to messy play very slowly and patiently in a small group. Some children may not make sound progress even with the provision of well-planned targeted interventions. They need specialist support.

Understanding the United Nations Convention on the Rights of the Child	• UNICEF in the United Kingdom have set out how the convention promotes and protects children's rights on their website.
Early disadvantage • The impact of early disadvantage • How to support children in danger of falling behind the majority	• The Early Intervention Foundation has systematically examined the research on quality in the Early Years, and how high-quality provision staffed by well-qualified practitioners can make a positive difference for disadvantaged children. • The Education Endowment Foundation has a wealth of free resources with a clear focus on effective support for disadvantaged children. • *Reducing educational disadvantage: a strategic approach in the early years* by Penny Tassoni (Bloomsbury Books, 2016)
Adverse Childhood Experiences (ACES): • What they are • How they can affect children	• The Marmot Report: Ten years on gives a brief summary of what ACEs are, and their prevalence, on pages 45–46. • The Early Intervention Foundation (2020) *Adverse childhood experiences: What we know, what we don't know, and what should happen next*
Promoting equal life chances: • Equality and diversity • Anti-racism • Unconscious bias	• The Equality and Human Rights Commission - *Research report 7: Early years, life chances and equality: a literature review* considers how early years experiences may affect the life chances of different groups of the population • Harvard University's EdCast: *Unconscious Bias in Schools* is a useful introduction. • *Young Children and Racial Justice* by Jane Lane (National Children's Bureau, 2008) • *Supporting you to raise anti-racist children* by Laura Henry-Allain and Emma Worrollo (Mattel, 2020)

Promoting equal life chances (cont.)	• The National Association for Special Educational Needs (NASEN) offers support and training for early years practitioners. • *Reasonable Adjustments in the early years* is a useful one-page guide from Norfolk Council.
The inclusion of children with SEND	• *The Inclusive Classroom Profile* by Elena P. Soukakou (Brookes Publishing, 2006) helps early years settings to check their inclusion. • Early Years Resources from the Autism Education Trust enable you to rate your practice and your setting overall. • *The SEN and Disability in the Early Years Toolkit* from the Council for Disabled Children supports early years settings in implementing the SEN and disability reforms.

HIGH-QUALITY CARE

- The child's experience must always be central to the thinking of every practitioner.

- Babies, toddlers and young children thrive when they are loved and well cared for.

- High-quality care is consistent. Every practitioner needs to enjoy spending time with young children.

- Effective practitioners are responsive to children and babies. They notice when a baby looks towards them and gurgles and respond with pleasure.

- Practitioners understand that toddlers are learning to be independent, so they will sometimes get frustrated.

- Practitioners know that starting school, and all the other transitions in the early years, are big steps for small children.

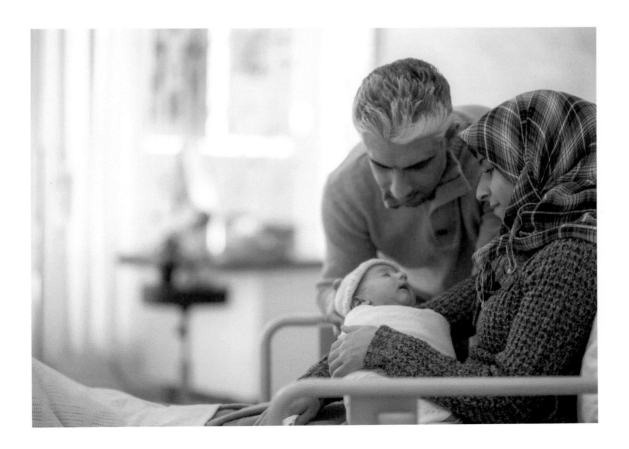

Babies, toddlers and young children in the early years need consistent, warm and responsive care from the adults they spend time with. Consistency matters for all children, and especially for the youngest.

The key person approach is a powerful way of ensuring that each child can be known, cared for and treasured by a special person. It's also an important way of ensuring that parents feel confident and know who to talk to if they have any concerns or important information to share.

An effective key person approach builds on attachment theory. Every child needs warm, loving and consistent care from their special adult. That strong relationship helps children to become more confident and to develop a wider web of relationships with other children and with adults. Key people can help young children to develop their awareness and understanding of their emotional states. In particular, elaborating on what children say about their feelings will help this development. So, when a child says *I'm sad*, the practitioner might elaborate on this by saying *I think you're sad because you couldn't have the car you wanted*.

Some children come into Early Years settings with emotions they might struggle to manage, such as anxiety, lack of confidence, shyness, anger, aggression or insecurity. This could be because of the temperament they were born with. Or, it could be because of a difficult earlier experience – for example, prematurity. This group of children in particular need key people and all staff to respond sensitively to their emotions. If responses are harsh or controlling, the children will not learn to develop positive behaviour. Instead, they may become aggressive and anti-social as they grow older. This risk is especially high for boys from disadvantaged backgrounds. So, it's important for teams to work together and support each other. Then responses to children with high levels of negative emotion can be calm and sympathetic, whilst boundaries and rules are applied consistently. Staff need to ensure that they do not respond by trying to over-direct and control the children. Over time, positive approaches will help the social development of all children, especially the most vulnerable.

The key person approach needs careful organisation and support from managers. Any close relationship can produce strong and sometimes difficult emotions. Key people need time and opportunities to talk through the complexities of their emotional work as carers. Whether an organisation cares for small children in the early years, or frail elderly people in a residential home, there is always a risk that the needs of the institution will come first.

Caring for young children is complex and demanding. There are no easy solutions to challenges like the need to respond warmly to all children, whatever our personal feelings may be. Or recognising that a 2-year-old's repeated tantrums are part of the child's healthy development. It's important that young children develop their independence, even though this might strain adults' patience.

The experience of the child must always be central to practitioners' thinking. This requires the organisation to take positive steps to make time for practitioners to reflect on the experiences of the children. Practitioners need to think about the 'child's voice'.

Transitions

Young children make many important transitions, such as their first experience of care outside the home when they join early education and care. Or the move from nursery into Reception. At all these points, children will be helped if settings and schools have clear procedures to support the transition. These might include:

- practitioners visiting children at home

- arrangements for children to visit their next setting with their parent and/or key person

- arrangements for the receiving practitioners to visit the child in their current setting.

It is crucial that everyone works together, in the best interests of the child, to make the transition as smooth as possible. Each person has valuable information to share about the child's strengths, and areas where extra help is needed. This will especially be the case if a child has SEND. Protocols for transition in neighbourhoods are useful. They can include agreed ways of summarising the child's development. For example, there could be a common report format which every setting uses. A local quality-assurance system can help to ensure that the reports are all written to a high-standard and are useful.

School readiness

There is no widely agreed definition of 'school readiness'. UNICEF (the United Nations Children's Fund) suggests that the three dimensions of school readiness are:

- children's readiness for school

- schools' readiness for children

- families' and communities' readiness for school.

School readiness: a conceptual framework (UNICEF, 2012)

When practitioners and parents work co-operatively, they can support the child through the process of transition in the best way possible. They can also ensure that the school is prepared for the child.

School readiness is about the skills and competencies the children have. It is also about their capacity, with support, to manage the transition into school. An effective focus on school readiness means that children are well prepared. They are ready to tackle the challenges they will face in the next phase of their education.

Implementing the key person approach and understanding attachment theory	• *Key Persons in the Early Years* by Peter Elfer, Elinor Goldschmied and Dorothy Selleck (Routledge, 2012) • *People Under Three: Play, Work and Learning in a Childcare Setting* by Sonia Jackson and Ruth Forbes (Routledge, 2014)
Effective approaches to supporting transitions in the early years	• *Supporting Transitions in the Early Years* by Liz Brooker (Open University Press, 2008) • *Improving School Transitions for Health Equity* (UCL Institute of Health Equity, 2015)

THE CURRICULUM: WHAT WE WANT CHILDREN TO LEARN

- The curriculum is a top-level plan of everything the early years setting wants the children to learn.

- Planning to help every child to develop their language is vital.

- The curriculum needs to be ambitious. Careful sequencing will help children to build their learning over time.

- Young children's learning is often driven by their interests. Plans need to be flexible.

- Babies and young children do not develop in a fixed way. Their development is like a spider's web with many strands, not a straight line.

- Depth in early learning is much more important than covering lots of things in a superficial way.

An early years curriculum provides a structure and sense of direction for the practitioners in the setting. It provides opportunities for all children to learn. It is ambitious. It challenges stereotypical beliefs that some groups of children are 'less able' to learn and make progress than others. It starts with children's experiences in their family and immediate environment, so learning is meaningful. Strong leadership is essential for the development, and monitoring, of a high-quality curriculum. The curriculum must be suitable for every child.

Leaders also need to support curriculum development with cycles of Professional Development. Some practitioners may also have gaps in their knowledge from their earlier training. They may need to know more about:

- how children develop and learn

- the best ways for adults to help them

- the key skills, concepts, communication skills and vocabulary that children need to learn at different ages.

It is important to avoid overloading the curriculum in the early years with too much content, especially for older children. This is a difficult balancing act. If there is too much to cover, then some children may struggle and start to fall behind. Careful curriculum design will help to ensure that all children keep up. It will ensure that some children will take part in additional rich, challenging and open-ended activities. They will experience curriculum content at greater depth. Other children will experience carefully planned and regular extra help, so they don't fall behind the majority.

It's important to value every child and believe that every child can make progress. When this is backed up by expert knowledge about how to support every child's learning, then early years education can promote equality and give every child a fair chance to succeed.

The diagram on the next page gives an example of a planning cycle. This is one way that settings might break their curriculum down into smaller units of planning:

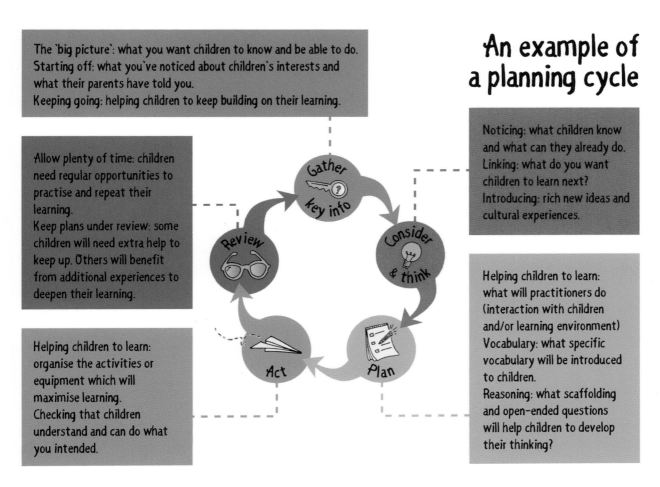

The 'big picture': what you want children to know and be able to do.
Starting off: what you've noticed about children's interests and what their parents have told you.
Keeping going: helping children to keep building on their learning.

An example of a planning cycle

Noticing: what children know and what can they already do.
Linking: what do you want children to learn next?
Introducing: rich new ideas and cultural experiences.

Allow plenty of time: children need regular opportunities to practise and repeat their learning.
Keep plans under review: some children will need extra help to keep up. Others will benefit from additional experiences to deepen their learning.

Gather key info

Review

Consider & think

Act

Plan

Helping children to learn: what will practitioners do (interaction with children and/or learning environment)
Vocabulary: what specific vocabulary will be introduced to children.
Reasoning: what scaffolding and open-ended questions will help children to develop their thinking?

Helping children to learn: organise the activities or equipment which will maximise learning.
Checking that children understand and can do what you intended.

Figure 3: An example of a planning and review cycle in the early years

Play is an essential part of the early years curriculum. That includes:

- play which is child-led: freely engaged in and enjoyed by children
- play which is sensitively supported and extended by adults
- play which is guided towards specific educational outcomes.

Free play is crucial to children's development. It's enjoyable and it helps children to develop their social skills and their self-regulation. Playing freely helps children to become more imaginative, more creative, and become better prepared to tackle difficult problems and solve them. High-quality play is supported by well-organised environments which respond to children's interests, and which widen those interests by introducing to children to new materials, experiences, activities and artistic expressions.

'The EPPSE Project found that children's play in the most effective settings was two thirds child-initiated and one third adult-initiated. In excellent settings, adults supported and extended children's self-initiated play more often. However, adults did not dominate the play. They backed off when children wanted to take over the play on their own.'

Effective pre-school, primary and secondary education project (EPPSE 3-16+)

(Taggart, B., Sylva, K., Melhuish, E., Sammons, P. and Siraj, I., 2015)

Play which is sensitively supported by adults is one of the key ways for young children to learn. As Professor Iram Siraj argues, 'play is widely recognised as a leading context for the child's acquisition of communication and collaboration skills' (Siraj, 2009, p. 80). For example, regular play with blocks helps children to develop their co-ordination. They have to place and balance blocks carefully to build structures. It also helps children to develop their attention: you have to concentrate hard to make sure that a tall tower doesn't tumble down!

As children make more complex structures with blocks, practitioners can point things out to them. They can use ordinary language to talk about the different shapes of blocks, words like 'curved', 'straight', 'thin' or 'long'. They can rephrase children's everyday language as mathematical language, for example refining 'big' to 'tall'. They can introduce early measurement concepts and ways of making comparisons, like 'taller than you' and 'shorter than you'. They can introduce counting and number concepts like 'one more'.

Sound curriculum design can also enhance the youngest children's play. An example of this is Treasure Basket play for babies who can sit up but not yet crawl. This gives babies a unique opportunity to explore different natural materials and to make choices about what they want to pick up and investigate more using their hands, mouths and all their senses. Practitioners need to prepare the resources and the learning environment carefully or the planned learning will not happen. The Treasure Baskets need to be made available to babies of the right age, in a protected space. Otherwise, the materials may be picked up by more confident toddlers and taken to different parts of the room.

Children often need rich first-hand experiences to play. After taking a small group of children on a bus ride, practitioners can enrich play back in the setting. That play could include important details like waiting at the bus-stop and checking the timetable. Children might pretend to buy tickets or use a smart card when they board. Rich play provides multiple opportunities for learning across all areas of the early years curriculum.

Settings will have some big goals for children, like learning to write in the Reception year. It's important to break down a large curricular goal like this. What are all of the essential things which a child must know and be able to do first? For example, in order to write a sentence, here are just some of the things which children need:

- The ability to speak in sentences. It is vital to support children's early communication before expecting them to write

- Motivation to write, when it's such a difficult skill for young children to learn

- Understanding of the features of print. For example, knowing that print has meaning and is written from left to right in English

- The physical skill to hold and control a pencil or pen.

A well-planned curriculum will map out the component skills children need to learn to write. It will emphasise developing children's communication and their physical skills. It will outline how children can have repeated, motivating experiences which help them to develop the skills they need. That will include the phonic knowledge they need to spell and the physical skills which lay the foundations for developing an efficient handwriting style. These skills need to be repeated over time until they become automatic. Each child needs to learn these skills in an appropriate sequence. It's no good expecting a child to *write* a sentence if they cannot *say* a sentence.

Development proceeds in a web of multiple strands

'New theories assume that development proceeds in a web of multiple strands, with different children following different pathways.'

Early Years Learning and Development Literature Review

(Evangelou, M., Sylva, K., Kyriacou, M., Wild, M. and Glenny, G., 2009)

Supporting the learning of young children is complex. It requires subtle professional skills. Whilst it is important to plan and offer the curriculum in a sequenced way, we would not expect young children to acquire skills and knowledge in exactly that order. That's why it's also so important for practitioners to notice children's learning and respond in the moment. That helps children to consolidate or extend their understanding and skills, and overcome struggles and difficulties.

Young children are often successful users of Information and Communication Technology (ICT). They quickly learn to switch between apps on phones and tablets, how to use the TV remote control, and how to take photos on a phone. This guidance considers ICT as a way to support children's learning and communication across all the different areas of learning. Children who are fascinated to see a snail in the garden might use the magnification app on a tablet to see its features in more detail. Children might take photos and videos as a way of recording their play, capturing a dance they have made up, or telling a story. They might switch between drawing with crayons and using their finger to draw on a tablet. A child might watch a cartoon online about a superhero, and then 'play out' what they've seen outdoors with their friends. ICT is not outlined as an area of development in its own right, but it has great potential to support children's learning when its use is carefully considered and planned. It can also be a particularly powerful tool for children with SEND. For example, children with spoken communication difficulties can be helped to communicate using specialist Alternative and Augmentative Communication (AAC) devices.

Curricular plans need regular review. Settings need a systematic approach to check that the curriculum is actually working to meet the needs of all the children. Children often attend two or more different settings in the EYFS: a child might start in a preschool and then move into a Reception class, for example. So, different providers in local areas need to work together. Then they can check that their work to promote the child's care and early learning leads to successful outcomes by the end of the Reception year.

Curricular plans will benefit from being flexible enough to allow for changes in direction. Practitioners need to respond quickly to children's sudden new interests.

A balance of deliberate teaching and spontaneous learning

'Without a balance of deliberate teaching and spontaneous learning, a "hands off" approach does not benefit children's learning. When teachers do not deliberately or intentionally extend children's interests and build on their learning over time, children are disadvantaged.'

Early mathematics: a guide for improving teaching and learning

(New Zealand Government Education Review Office, 2016)

Young children benefit from a balanced curriculum which includes teaching that's been planned ahead, and also makes time for their spontaneous learning. They need organised, adult-guided learning to bring new ideas and experiences into their lives. They need well-planned, specific learning experiences. These will deepen or consolidate their learning over time. Otherwise, children will miss out on valuable learning.

Research published by the Department for Education (*Children's Experiences of the Early Years Foundation Stage* by Garrick and others, 2010) found that children enjoy planning their activities. But children say that they are not as involved in the planning process as they could be. They say that they enjoy real-world activities and experiences in early years settings. These experiences include cleaning, gardening, shopping and food preparation. They also value visits beyond their setting, like going to a place of interest or to see a show. Activities like these can stimulate particularly varied and rich conversations.

As you get to know families, you may find that some children have not yet experienced many of these trips. They may never have been to the park, or into a natural area like a forest or a beach. Some children haven't been to museums or been in the audience for a live music, dance or theatrical performance. Early years settings, in partnership with parents, can do a great deal to enrich young children's lives further.

The guidance in *Development Matters* broadly outlines children's typical learning at different ages. That's intended to help practitioners and settings with their curricular planning. It can help practitioners to consider which goals might be important in a child's development. *Development Matters* can support, but cannot replace, practitioners' wider expertise, knowledge of child development and professional judgement.

'Intentional teaching means teachers act with specific outcomes or goals in mind for children's development and learning. Teachers must know when to use a given strategy to accommodate the different ways that individual children learn and the specific content they are learning.'

The intentional teacher: choosing the best strategies for young children's learning

(Epstein, A., 2007)

It is useful to reflect on how we can check that children's knowledge and skills are secure at earlier stages, before trying to 'move them on'. For example, practitioners working with Reception-age children are advised to check all of the earlier stages of development. It's important to ensure that every child's learning is secure first, rather than go straight to the Reception year guidance.

The Early Learning Goals are a brief check of some of the important skills and concepts children should have by the end of the Reception year. They are not a curriculum.

Young children's development is not orderly: different children follow different pathways. That's one of the key reasons why practitioners need to be cautious about the idea of 'readiness'. If we wait until we see spontaneous signs of 'readiness' in a child's freely chosen play, that child might well miss out on a lot of the help they need to learn.

Young children think and reason like adults, but they are inexperienced. There are many things they have not done, seen or practised yet. So rather than waiting for children to be ready, it's important for practitioners to ensure that children have all the experiences they need to make progress from their current level of development. It's not helpful to wait for a child to be ready to write. Nor is it helpful to expect them to write when they can't. But, by giving a child lots of support with their communication, lots of experiences to develop the physical skills they need, and lots of motivating reasons to write, we can help them to make progress.

Depth in learning is much more important than breadth. Deep understanding is more important than superficial coverage.

Effective approaches to leading and evaluating the early years curriculum	Curriculum, Leadership and Interaction Quality Rating Scales (CLIQRS): the UK family of rating scales published by the UCL-IOE Press • ECERS-E (2010) by Kathy Sylva, Iram Siraj and Brenda Taggart • SSTEW (2015) by Iram Siraj, Denise Kingston and Edward Melhuish • MOVERS (2017) by Carol Archer and Iram Siraj
Effective practice: supporting children's early learning, including communication, language, literacy and maths	• *Making play work for education* (2015) by Weisberg, D.S. and others • *Preparing for Literacy: Improving Communication, Language and Literacy in the Early Years* (Education Endowment Foundation, 2018) • *Improving Mathematics in the Early Years and Key Stage 1* (Education Endowment Foundation, 2020)

PEDAGOGY: HELPING CHILDREN TO LEARN

- Children are powerful learners. Every child can make progress in their learning, with the right help.

- Effective pedagogy is a mix of different approaches. Children learn through play, by adults modelling, by observing each other, and through guided learning and direct teaching.

- Practitioners carefully organise enabling environments for high-quality play. Sometimes, they make time and space available for children to invent their own play. Sometimes, they join in to sensitively support and extend children's learning.

- Children in the early years also learn through group work, when practitioners guide their learning.

- Older children need more of this guided learning.

- A well-planned learning environment, indoors and outside, is an important aspect of pedagogy.

Babies, toddlers and young children are naturally curious. They love to explore, play, communicate and learn. They are, as the leading child development researcher Alison Gopnik says, 'the best learning machines in the universe'.

Adults can help children to learn in many encouraging, thoughtful and gently challenging ways. This help needs to take place across the whole range of contexts and areas of learning. These include:

- creating a rich and stimulating environment, indoors and outside, so that children can choose their own play and activities

- joining in with children's play when appropriate, and sensitively introducing challenges and new ideas

- setting challenges for children in a sensitive way and allowing them to find their own solutions to problems

- showing children how to do things (modelling) and explaining how to do things

- encouraging children to collaborate and learn from each other

- guiding children's learning in a playful way

- discussing ideas with children, using skilful questioning and challenging their thinking to help them clarify their understanding of ideas

- commenting on what children are doing

- directly teaching children a new skill, concept or an important piece of information

- using ICT to support children's learning, using the approaches set out above.

Pedagogy is the technical term for all the different ways that practitioners help children to learn, and how they teach them. Practitioners need a wide range of different pedagogical strategies to draw on. It's a bit like being an actor who can play many different parts. Effective settings provide a balance between play activities, which children choose to take part, and practitioner-led group activities. Settings will use their professional judgement to work out the balance that works best for them. They will need to take account of the particular strengths and needs of the children they are working with.

An important aspect of pedagogy is checking what children know and can do. This is discussed in detailed in the section below on *Assessment*. In daily practice, effective pedagogy and assessment go hand in hand.

Scaffolding

One of the most powerful ways to help children's learning is 'scaffolding'. The idea behind scaffolding is that each child has two levels of development:

- what they can do on their own

- what they can do with the help of another person.

For example, a child may not be able to complete a jigsaw on their own. But they might be able to do the puzzle if a practitioner provides sensitive challenge, support and guidance. The practitioner could perhaps draw the child's attention to how turning a piece might be needed for it to fit, or highlight the colours of different pieces.

This approach draws on the work of the great Russian theorist Lev Vygotsky. He argued that teaching should always be aimed at the child's emerging skills, not at the existing ones (Vygotsky, 1978).

Vygotsky called the space where the child's skills are emerging the 'zone of proximal development'

Zone of proximal development

Figure 4: The Zone of Proximal Development

When young children are learning to tackle new problems, scaffolding is an effective approach. It means giving children just enough help to do something which they could not do alone. Over time, the help is gradually reduced until children can solve the problem themselves. For example, at first a baby can reach for socks and grab them, but cannot pull them onto her feet. The practitioner can guide the baby's hand and encourage the baby to help in pulling the sock on, too.

Throughout the early years, practitioners can use this approach. For example, you could encourage children to be active in nappy-changing routines (e.g. taking off their shoes themselves). Over time, babies and toddlers can co-operate more and more with nappy-changing. In the long term, this will help them to become independent in dressing and undressing. It will also help them when they are learning to use the toilet independently. You can use scaffolding as well to help a child learn how to put their coat on and do it up. For example, you might encourage children to pull up the zip after you have started them off. Over time, through modelling and encouragement, children will learn to engage and pull up the zip themselves.

Practitioners need to think carefully about these interactions. If too much help is provided, the child won't learn, and may start to become dependent on adults. If you do up the zip of a toddler's coat every day, they'll never learn to do it themselves. But if a child doesn't know *how* to pull their zip up and you just tell them to 'try again', they are most likely to become frustrated. Over time, some children who are thrown back on their resources like that might lose confidence in themselves.

Extension and elaboration are especially helpful for babies, toddlers and young children. For example, if a small child says *car*, the practitioner can say *the car's driving along*. If a child says they are sad, the practitioner can engage the child in some conversation. Why are they sad? What could they do, to make themselves feel calmer or happier? When children are confidently using a tool like scissors, practitioners can extend the children's skills. They can show children how another tool, like a hole-puncher, is used. Then they can encourage the children to use it independently.

Skilful early years practitioners are constantly judging when to step in and scaffold further. Sometimes it's best to step back and scaffold by doing nothing more than making encouraging noises to show interest.

The diagram below summarises some scaffolding techniques. These can help children to develop their independence and become more powerful learners.

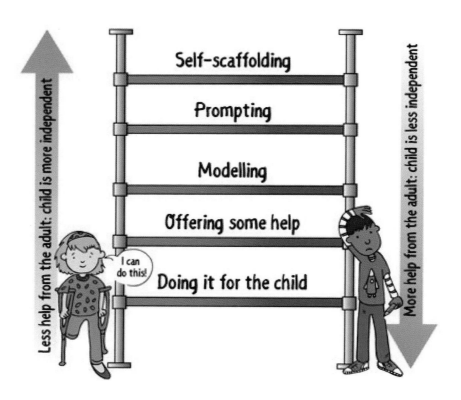

Figure 5: Scaffolding techniques in the early years

Self-scaffolding. Self-scaffolding represents the highest level of children's independence. Practitioners observe and give children plenty of time for to try different ways of doing things, and for thinking. Self-scaffolders can plan how to approach a task; problem-solve as they go; and review how they approached a task.

Prompting. Practitioners might provide prompts when children don't self-scaffold. Prompts encourage children to keep trying, without telling them exactly what to do. The aim is to nudge children into using a self-scaffolding technique. For example: *What do you need to do first? How do you think you could join them together? What worked for you last time? Keep going, you can do this!*

Modelling. Prompts won't work if a child needs a new skill. Practitioners sometimes need to model or demonstrate what to do. For example: *knead the dough like this* or *pull up on the zip like I'm doing.* Children need to try the same step for themselves immediately afterwards, so they can practise and learn it.

Offering some help. Sometimes a little bit of help supports a child to keep doing. For example: *If I do that piece of the jigsaw, you do this one* or *How about I write the first letter of your name, then you do the rest?*

Doing it for the child. Small children can't manage everything, so they need practitioners to do some things for them. Even so, practitioners can encourage them to join in. Babies can be given the nappy to hold during their nappy-change, for example. Children of all ages in the early years sometimes need a lot of help. They might be tired, or generally having a bad day. It can be nice when someone makes you a cup of tea, even though you can do it yourself. In the same way, sometimes it's important to do things for a child. A bit of kindness can help a child through a difficult patch.

Sustained shared thinking

A practice which is related to scaffolding is **Sustained Shared Thinking**. This is 'an episode in which two or more individuals "work together" in an intellectual way to solve a problem, clarify a concept, evaluate activities, extend a narrative etc. Both parties must contribute to the thinking and it must develop and extend' (Siraj-Blatchford and others, 2002, p. 8)

This generally happens in one-to-one adult/child interactions. Research into Sustained Shared Thinking shows that it occurs rarely, and is found in the highest-quality early years settings.

A few 4-year-olds were sitting together. Three of the children were wearing trainers that would light up when they stepped down on them.

Teacher: Wow! Look at your shoes! That is so cool. They light up when you step down.

Child 1: Yes, they do this. [Jumps up and down several times]

Teacher: How does that happen? How does it light up?

Child 1: Because they are new.

Teacher: Um. Mine are new too but they don't light up.

Child 2: No, because they light up when you step down on them. [Steps down hard several times]

Teacher: [Steps down hard several times] That's funny. Mine don't light up when I step down.

Child 3: No, no, no, you have to have these holes [points to the holes]

Teacher: [Pointing to the holes in her own shoe] But I have holes and mine still don't light up, and Josh has holes in his trainers too and his do not light up either. I wonder why?

Child 4: I think you need batteries. Kids, you need batteries.

Child 1: Yeah, you need batteries to make them work. [Thinks for a while]. But I did not see batteries when I put my toes in.

Child 4: I think they are under the toes.

Child 2: I can't feel the batteries under my toes. Teacher: I wonder how we can find out about this?

From a 2016 PowerPoint presentation by Kathy Sylva to the Transatlantic Forum on Inclusive Early Years

Tuning in.

Listening carefully to what is being said, observing body language and what the child is doing

Showing genuine interest:

giving our whole attention, maintaining eye contact, affirming, smiling, nodding

respecting children's own decisions and choices inviting children to elaborate: I really want to know more about this.

Re-capping: *So, you think that...*

Offering our own experience: *I like to listen to music when I cook supper at home.*

Clarifying ideas: *Right, Darren, so you think that this stone will melt if I boil it in water?*

Suggesting: *You might like to try doing it this way.*

Reminding: *Don't forget that you said that this stone will melt if I boil it.*

Using encouragement to further thinking: *You have really thought hard about where to put this door in the palace but where on earth will you put the windows?*

Offering an alternative viewpoint: *Maybe Goldilocks wasn't naughty when she ate the porridge?*

Speculating: *Do you think the three bears would have liked Goldilocks to come to live with them as their friend?*

Reciprocating: *Thank goodness that you were wearing wellington boots when you jumped in those puddles, Kwame! Look at my feet; they are soaking wet.*

Asking open questions: *How did you? Why does this…? What happens next? What do you think?*

Modelling thinking: *I have to think hard about what I do this evening. I need to take my dog to the vet's because he has a sore foot, take my library books back to the library and buy some food for dinner tonight. But I just won't have time to do all of these things.*

From a 2005 PowerPoint presentation by Iram Siraj to the TACTYC Annual Conference

It is important for practitioners to focus on the processes children follow in their learning, and the effort they show. This helps to build children's character and confidence. It encourages them to try new and challenging things. On the other hand, too much praise can be unhelpful. It encourages children to take part in unchallenging activities because they can get a reward, like being told they're 'good' or getting a sticker.

To develop their ability to keep going when learning is hard, and to bounce back after failures, children need to be sensitively challenged. The 2-year-old struggling to climb up an A-frame will experience a deep satisfaction when they finally get to the top. It will be the same for the 4-year-old who finally manages to ride a bike without stabilisers. Or the 5-year-old who manages to read a whole sentence for the first time, unaided.

Practitioners can help children to become more powerful learners by setting challenges that are just a bit beyond what a child can easily do. Children may need plenty of encouragement to keep trying. Without challenges, some children won't progress well. A child may have enjoyed pedalling a three-wheeled trike around the nursery garden at three, and benefited from the experience. If they are still just pedalling a three-wheeled trike around in Reception, they are not getting the support they need to make progress. Repeating low-level activities will not help children to learn about the importance of continual practice and improvement.

Children of all ages need time to choose their play and other activities freely. High-quality resources which are carefully selected and arranged will ensure that their play is rich in potential learning. There are also times when children need practitioners to start things off for them. They need lots of playful, practitioner-guided activities. There is a role for adults to take the initiative at every stage in the early years. Key people in the baby room will start up games of 'Peepo'. Practitioners in Reception classes will work with groups of children on a systematic phonics programme. Older children in the EYFS need more of this adult-guided group learning.

In Expressive Arts and Design, children need opportunities to make their own choices. They benefit from practitioner-guidance and direct teaching, together with plenty of time and opportunities to explore materials and equipment. Children learn about the nature of paint through repeatedly touching, finger-painting and using paintbrushes. They find out about how paint drips and smudges, how colours change when they are combined. They see that the paper will get soggy and will eventually tear if you keep adding paint.

Teaching children skills, and making sure they have plenty of time to practise, can help them to develop their creativity. You may be able to express a wider range of ideas through dance once you know more dance moves. You may become more creative in your singing after you've practised a song lots of times, and know it well. Then, with encouragement, you can improvise around what you know and make up your own variations. However, there is a need for balance. Children's movement and dance can also be developed through adults imitating their movements and, when appropriate, extending them. That way children create their own moves. Over-practice can kill off all the joy in dance and singing. It's important, and fascinating, to notice and celebrate children's vocalisations in their free play.

It is important to stress the role that the learning environment plays in early years pedagogy. High-quality, challenging learning materials can be stored so that children can access them and use them regularly in open-ended ways. Both indoors and outside, resources like these help children to challenge and extend their learning over time. Children will need lots of adult guidance to learn how to manage this type of learning environment. They will need to learn about keeping spaces tidy and organised, so that others can play there. Approaches like Forest School and Beach School give children exciting and challenging contexts for learning outdoors, taking measured risks, and developing a love of nature.

Children say that varied and flexible resources and a relatively large open area help them to identify a wider range of play interests and more complex play. For example, a pretend pirate ship outdoors may only ever be a pirate ship. The children might get bored with that theme. On the other hand, hollow blocks, empty cardboard boxes, planks and material can be endlessly changed – to a pirate ship, a bus or the cave in *We're Going on a Bear Hunt*.

Environmental Rating Scales can help settings to evaluate their learning environment. These can play an important part in checking the quality and impact of resources, equipment, routines, structure, and pedagogy.

Ways to evaluate the effectiveness of pedagogy for children in the early years	• *ITERS-3* (2017) by Noreen Yazejian, Thelma Harms, Richard M. Clifford and Debby Cryer (Teachers' College Press) • *ECERS-3* (2014) by Thelma Harms, Richard M. Clifford and Debby Cryer (Teachers' College Press) • *FCCERS-3* (2019) by Noreen Yazejian, Thelma Harms, Richard M. Clifford and Debby Cryer (Teachers' College Press) • *ECERS-E* (2010) by Kathy Sylva, Iram Siraj and Brenda Taggart (Trentham Books)
What the international evidence says about quality in early childhood education and care: delivery, pedagogy and child outcomes	• *Fostering Effective Early Learning Study: A review of the current international evidence considering quality in early childhood education and care programmes* (2017) by Iram Siraj and others

ASSESSMENT: CHECKING WHAT CHILDREN HAVE LEARNT

- Assessment is about noticing what children can do and what they know. It is not about lots of data and evidence.

- Effective assessment requires practitioners to understand child development. Practitioners also need to be clear about what they want children to know and be able to do.

- Accurate assessment can highlight whether a child has a special educational need and needs extra help.

- Before assessing children, it's a good idea to think about whether the assessments will be useful.

- Assessment should not take practitioners away from the children for long periods of time.

Accurate assessment is essential to high-quality early years education and care.

As practitioners, we make hundreds, if not thousands, of assessments every day we work with children.

When we decide which child needs our help to pour a cup of water, and which child can do it on their own, we are making assessments. When we give a child just enough help to pour from a jug, we are using assessment to decide on the best response. This is known as formative assessment. These kinds of assessments inform the decisions that practitioners make, minute by minute. They are rarely written down or recorded.

On other occasions it is very important to make a note of assessments. Children have a very wide range of starting points when they come into the early years. So, it is important to assess their level of development on entry. This is done best when it's in partnership with parents and anyone else working with the child (for example, a health visitor, or a speech therapist). Without that initial assessment, it is not possible to check that each child is making the best progress they are capable of. We need to find out if some children have barriers to their learning, too. So, it's important to check which children may not be making progress.

Practitioners have to make complex decisions about assessment, drawing on their expertise and professionalism. When we are noticing what children can and cannot do, and they are changing rapidly, we have to jot down notes. It will not be possible to remember all this information at the end of a busy day. So, practitioners will need to keep records. It may be helpful to think about this as keeping records on some of the children, some of the time, but not all of the children, all of the time. Some children may require more detailed records than others. When parents and children are involved in these processes, assessments will be richer and more rounded.

Providing a supporting and stimulating environment

'Formative assessment will lie at the heart of providing a supporting and stimulating environment for every child. This may require professional development for practitioners and liaison with individuals and agencies outside the setting.'

Early Years Learning and Development Literature Review

(Evangelou, M., Sylva, K., Kyriacou, M., Wild, M. and Glenny, G., 2009)

Ongoing information is needed to inform the type of assessment which sums up a child's learning, development and health at a particular time. There are two legally required summative assessment reports during the early years. They are the Statutory Check at Two, and the Early Years Foundation Stage Profile. Summative assessment supports children at other transition points, too. An example of this would be a child's move from a nursery setting into a Reception class.

Assessment is most effective when it guides professional judgement. For example, we need to check that we are not making assumptions about children which later turn out to be wrong. The child who sits nicely and appears to listen at story time may not be understanding enough to make sense of the book. Equally, other children may appear distracted on occasion, but actually be learning well over time.

But there is no reason for assessment to replace professional judgement. For example, children may make progress unevenly. A period of 'no progress' may actually be an important time for the child to consolidate and repeat what they already know and can do. It does not make sense to expect every child to make regular steps of progress according to a particular schedule.

There is also no need for assessment to take up so much time that it interferes with caring for children, teaching them or playing with them. It's often more sensible to keep engaged with children when they are doing something really significant – to continue the conversation or give them the encouragement they need to keep on trying. Practitioners can always make a note about children's significant learning after the event.

It's also important to beware of the danger of jumping in with an assessment before giving children the help they need to learn. It's common to ask children questions like *how many blocks have you got there?* Before asking a question like this, it is worth considering how much help you've given the children to learn about number and counting. Are you regularly drawing their attention to the number of things throughout the day and during ordinary routines? Children and adults can usefully count the cups for the snack table, or check that all the pencils are in the pot at tidy-up time, for example.

Before collecting assessments, practitioners can useful ask themselves 'why'? How will they use the information? It's important to have a clear purpose in mind. Throughout the year, assessment information is needed. It's a way of ensuring that planning, resources and routines are right for the children on roll. For example, many children might enter a nursery class and have levels of development which are lower than expected for 3-year-olds. In that case, the nursery provision will need to be geared so that the children make rapid progress. At first, it will look more like provision for two-year olds, and less like a nursery class for 3-year olds. There will be a strong focus on the three prime areas of learning. There will be many opportunities for children to develop their communication and their physical skills.

Helpful assessments will pinpoint how well a child is progressing towards the setting's curricular goals. They will guide planning, routines and resourcing. But they are not helpful if they apply fixed ability-categories to children which limit their future learning. Development moves quickly when children are young: for example, many children with early language difficulties will be communicating appropriately by the time they leave the early years. Two and 3-year-olds with language difficulties are not 'low ability'. They will not learn well if they are grouped in such a way that they miss out on enriching story times and other activities. Similarly, the development of summer-born children is likely to be behind those children born in the autumn. That does not mean that they have difficulties in learning, just that they are younger. They need a broad and stimulating range of activities just like any other children.

'Many respondents also voiced concerns that paperwork demands are negatively impacting on the amount and/or quality of time they are able to spend with the children in their care. One stated: "The red tape and paperwork has become over the top, which means the staff spend half their time filling in paperwork, instead of what really matters which is of course the children. This leads to staff taking work home."'

Minds Matter: the impact of working in the early years sector on practitioners' mental health and wellbeing

Early Years Alliance (2018)

Most children will make sound progress, given favourable circumstances at home and in their setting. It is not necessary to track lots of examples of their learning and progress. In fact, the work involved in doing that can damage practitioners' wellbeing. It can stop practitioners from spending time with the children and helping them to learn new things.

Assessment is about individual children and their learning, not rows and rows of data. It's about knowing which children are getting on well, so that they can continue to be challenged and stimulated. It's about everyone in a setting knowing which children might be at risk of poor progress, and giving them extra help when it's needed. It's not about amassing 'evidence'. Larger settings will need appropriate and manageable ways of measuring and organising assessment information. They need to make sure that no group of children is being disadvantaged (e.g. boys and girls, or children from specific ethnic groups).

Children who are not making progress

Over time, some children may appear not to be making progress. For example, many children learning English as an additional language have a 'silent phase' when they are listening and watching. During that time, they don't yet feel confident to speak in English. This is an expected pattern of development. But a few children learning English as an additional language will have a 'silent phase' that goes on for much longer than usual. Similarly, because learning to count is tricky, many children will get muddled at first. They might get their numbers in the wrong order. Sometimes they might say numbers in the right order, but without one-to-one correspondence. But a few children will have longer-term difficulties in learning to count accurately from 1 to 5.

In these cases, it is important that practitioners use detailed and diagnostic assessment. This group of children is more in need of assessment work than others in the group. The parent of the child making poor progress learning English may explain that their child's home language seems delayed, too. That might lead to a referral to a Speech and Language Therapist.

In the case of a child who is struggling to learn to count, more detailed assessment might pinpoint their difficulty. Perhaps they don't yet understand that the last number word you say represents the number of the group. So, the child might simply say *1 - 2 - 3 - 4 - 5*. The practitioner may need to use a quiet space with few distractions and focus on counting up to three for a period of time. That may be enough to help the child consolidate their understanding. Or it might be that the child's difficulty is attention: they are looking around and getting involved in many different things. This means they are not yet able to concentrate on counting. In this case, the practitioner might help the child to build up their attention span through using finger rhymes. Regular play with cause-and-effect toys can also help. With the practitioner's support, the child can enjoy careful watching and waiting for the exciting moment that the Jack-in-a-Box pops up!

Careful assessment can help children overcome short-term difficulties in their learning. It guides practitioners to plan the appropriate extra help. That might involve giving children extra attention during their regular play and activities. Or it might involve planning and offering children small-group interventions which are led by a highly skilled practitioner. All of these approaches will help children to keep up with the others in their group.

Sometimes, careful assessment by practitioners is not able to pinpoint a child's barriers to learning. In those cases, the child and their family will need a referral to a specialist service. For example, more than 10% of children and young people will have persistent and long-term speech, language and communication needs. They need early and ongoing access to specialist help, including speech and language therapy.

Effective early years practitioners are a bit like the harbour master who keeps an eye on the boats as they come into the harbour. Most boats are heading safely into dock, although they are going at different rates and following different courses. The harbour master does not need to watch every single one every moment of the day. But some boats may be going off course, or perhaps they won't make it into the dock that day. Those are the boats the harbour master needs to pay extra attention to, because they need extra help in order to dock safely.

That attention cannot be limited to just one point in time. Practitioners will be checking later on whether the help has worked, or whether more or a different form of help might be needed.

Children can make good use of assessment information when it is shared with them. It can help them to remember their previous learning. It can give them an opportunity to talk about how they learn best. It can enable them to see how they are becoming more powerful learners, as they develop more skills and learn new things. Some children say that they do not think the record-keeping undertaken in settings is 'their own'. They say that they are unhappy that they cannot understand the written information.

Equality and diversity

Finally, there are important issues to consider around equalities and diversity in the area of assessment. For example, there are some worrying government statistics about children's achievements in the Early Years Foundation Stage. Children from some ethnic groups have higher attainment than others by the end of the Early Years Foundation Stage. Gypsy and Irish Traveller children have particularly low attainment. Early intervention, in partnership with parents, is essential. It can make a vital difference to children, or groups of children, who are at risk of making poor progress.

There are also significant issues to consider in relation to many other groups. Two examples are the progress and attainment of boys with special educational needs, and children who are eligible for free school meals. Sometimes, issues are local, not national. Children from a particular ethnic group might be doing well nationally. But in a particular setting, or local authority, they might not be doing so well.

Disadvantages can also overlap. Boys from a particular ethnic group might not be making sound progress. But the data for that group overall does not look concerning, because girls are doing so much better. It is important to look carefully at assessment data in the provision, locally and nationally. Practitioners, especially leaders, might consider how they can use assessment information to ask themselves difficult questions. How well is the provision meeting the needs of all children?

It's also useful for practitioners to consider whether they notice confident and talkative children more. Do they write more observations about this group of children, and in turn is there more planning that supports their interests and their needs? If that is the case, then other children might be missing out. If they are left out, they might be left behind.

Children who can easily be left behind include those who are quieter, shyer or less confident in communicating in English. Research suggests that some children's learning is often overlooked. This can affect children who spend more time outdoors and are mostly involved in physical, fast-moving play. It can also affect children who do not make things that represent their learning like drawings, painting and models.

Effective use of assessment helps practitioners to identify whether particular children, or groups of children, are at risk of poor progress. This includes ongoing, formative assessment. It also includes summative assessment, like the Progress Check at Two or the Early Years Foundation Stage Profile.

It's always worthwhile to reflect on the ways they interact with children, set up the provision and make assessments. Are we being fair to all children? We need to act promptly on such reflections, and on assessment information, to promote equality. High-quality early education and care can play a part in building a fairer society for all children.

Some children may appear to be struggling with their learning and development. They may often seem to be very angry, or withdrawn. They may find it difficult to engage positively in play, or find it unusually distressing to switch from one activity to another. They may be in danger of falling behind the majority of children.

In-depth assessment can help practitioners to clarify their concerns, discuss children's difficulties with parents, and involve other professionals.

Settings may want to consider using the evidence-informed Early Years Toolbox. This is a suite of iPad-based assessments which are suitable for early years settings to use with young children. The assessments focus on the areas of learning which research suggests are the best predictors of later success in school and life.

Communication	*Universally Speaking* from the Communication Trust outlines the stages of children's communication development from birth to 5 years
Personal, social and emotional development	The *Strengths and Difficulties Questionnaire (SDQ)* is a brief emotional and behavioural screening questionnaire for children and young people.
Physical development	When children are 2, health visitors carry out the *Ages and Stages Questionnaire (ASQ-3)*. This includes a check on the child's gross and fine motor skills. If you are worried about a child's physical development, ask their parent to share their ASQ or ask for permission to contact their health visitor.
Children's views about assessment	Flewitt, P. and Cowan, K. (2020) *Valuing Young Children's Signs of Learning: Observation and Digital Documentation of Play in Early Years Classrooms*

.

SELF-REGULATION AND EXECUTIVE FUNCTION

Executive function includes the child's ability to:

- hold information in mind
- focus their attention
- regulate their behaviour
- plan what to do next.

These abilities contribute to the child's growing ability to self-regulate:

- focus their thinking
- monitor what they are doing and adapt
- regulate strong feelings
- be patient for what they want
- bounce back when things get difficult.

Language development is central to self-regulation: children use language to guide their actions and plans. Pretend play gives many opportunities for children to focus their thinking, persist and plan ahead.

Executive function and self-regulation skills

'Executive function and self-regulation skills are the mental processes that enable us to plan, focus attention, remember instructions, and juggle multiple tasks successfully. Just as an air traffic control system at a busy airport safely manages the arrivals and departures of many aircraft on multiple runways, the brain needs this skill set to filter distractions, prioritize tasks, set and achieve goals, and control impulses.'

Center on the Developing Child, Harvard University

If you pause for a moment to reflect, it's clear that these skills are essential for children's learning and healthy development. For example, if a child can't manage to filter distractions, they will find it very difficult to sustain their involvement in learning and play. As a result, they may appear to be more preoccupied with what's going on around them, as they flit from one thing to the next.

Children develop these different types of self-regulation to differing extents. So, a child may be very good at cognitive and behavioural self-regulation but not so good at emotional self-regulation. These differences are largely dependent upon the child's previous experiences. Important early experiences include having conversations and playing with adults and other children.

Executive function refers to basic cognitive operations, particularly attention control, short-term (working) memory, and inhibition. The development of inhibition means that whilst a child might wish to grab a toy off another, they will inhibit that desire and wait their turn.

A child who has good executive function and has the experiences that foster self-regulation is very likely to develop good self -regulation. Self-regulation develops as an interaction of executive function and experience.

If a child had good executive function but does not have such good self-regulation experiences, they may not develop good self-regulation.

Executive function is largely controlled by basic maturation of the nervous system.

Children are not born with self-regulation skills. They develop them as they experience warm, nurturing and loving relationships with important adults and others. Clear, sensible and consistent behavioural boundaries are also important.

Success not just in school, but in life

'Central to development are the executive functions of the brain, which encompass cognitive flexibility, inhibition and working memory, as well as more complex functions such as capacities to problem solve, reason and plan. Self-regulation is the primary characteristic of these higher mental functions, supporting the qualities of creativity, flexibility and self-control, all of which begin to develop during early childhood — qualities which are crucial for success not just in school, but in life. Skills involved with self-regulation - such as executive functioning and attention control - are also necessary to build healthy and positive relationships with other people.'

Getting it right in the Early Years Foundation Stage: a review of the evidence

Pascal, C., Bertram, T. and Rouse, L. (2020)

Adverse circumstances can make it more difficult for some children to develop their self-regulation skills. For example, a child growing up in overcrowded housing may be in a constantly noisy environment. The child might struggle to focus their attention onto one person talking.

The good news is that high-quality early years provision can make a powerful difference to all children. It is especially helpful for children facing disadvantage. It helps them to develop their self-regulation and executive function skills.

When a practitioner scaffolds a task, this helps children to develop these skills. For example, some young children may struggle to cut off a piece of sticky tape to join two boxes together. The tape is hard to cut, and then it might curl over and stick to itself whilst the child positions the boxes together.

Scaffolding might involve recognising the child's feelings: 'this is making you feel cross. That's OK. Let's see what you can do to solve the problem'. Scaffolding by the adult might then involve breaking the task down into smaller components. Perhaps the adult might show the child how to cut the tape off and stick it to the edge of the table, ready to use, so it does not twist over. Next, the adult might suggest positioning the boxes together and might offer to hold them still whilst the child applies the tape.

All of these actions help children to learn cognitive and behavioural self-regulation. They give children examples of how to focus on specific aspects of the situation and to plan a sequence of behaviours. They help children to attend to a task in a systematic way, with a goal in mind and to focus their attention. Children also learn other valuable lessons. lessons. It is natural to feel angry when frustrated - but they can handle those feelings and go back to a difficult task in an organised way and try again. That's an example of emotional self-regulation.

Plan-do-review

Similarly, as children plan how they will take part in activities, they are developing their self-regulation. Practitioners can use scaffolding to support this, like a 'plan–do–review' approach. This might involve a practitioner talking children through their 'plans' for their play. Then children will think ahead about the resources they need and what they will be doing. This can help them screen out other distractions at the 'do' phase, and focus their attention. The conversation with the practitioner at the 'review' stage can help the child to think about which of their ideas worked. They might think about what they would do differently next time.

'Plan–do–review' cycles can be structured, for example by using approaches from the American High/Scope or Tools of the Mind programmes. Or, they can be more flexible and informal. As a child approaches the block area, the practitioner might engage them in a brief conversation about what they are planning to make. Once the structure is completed, the practitioner might develop a conversation with the child about what they have built and encourage them to talk about what they think of their building. In that way, they have completed an informal cycle of 'plan–do–review'.

Clear boundaries for behaviour can also help children to develop self-regulation. Boundaries must be appropriate to the children's ages and levels of development. Practitioners can support children's social development by seeing ordinary conflicts and difficulties as opportunities for children to learn. They are not merely times when children need telling off. For example, if a 2-year-old snatches a toy from another child, the practitioner might intervene and comfort the child who has lost the toy. Then they might restore the toy to its rightful owner. That could be followed by the practitioner showing the child a better way to handle that situation next time. For example, the practitioner might say, *Next time, you could say 'can I have a turn next?' – shall we practise that now?*

Over time, children internalise the ways of behaviour that are modelled for them by adults. This helps them to develop their emotional self-regulation. Then they can begin to follow routines and boundaries for themselves, without needing to be told. Children who keep muttering *my turn next, my turn next* as they fidget and wait near the top of the steps to the slide are self-regulating. They are beginning to control their emotions and their impulses to push their way to the top. They are internalising the idea that if you wait, you will have a turn.

Self-regulation and co-regulation

Young children need some regulation by others, or 'co-regulation'. An example of this is when an adult and child adapt to each other's emotions. This happens when the adult tunes in to the child's emotions. For example, if the child is sad, the adult is sympathetic and supportive. This is a way that adults can help children to manage their impulses, anger or distress. Emotional self-regulation means experiencing, and also managing your feelings.

If young children don't feel emotionally safe, and are not helped with emotional self-regulation, they will struggle to learn. As Usha Goswami explains, findings from neuroscience tell us that 'good instructional practice can be undermined by brain-based factors such as learning anxiety, attention deficits and poor recognition of social cues. All of these factors disrupt an individual's capacity to learn, and also have an effect on other learners'.

Scaffolding in such situations involves explaining why it is important to take turns, and why it is important not to upset others. For that to be effective, the child must have a warm and trusting relationship with the adult in the first place. There has to be an all-round spirit of friendly co-operation. Practitioners can be sympathetic to the wishes and impulses of young children, as they help them learn to regulate their emotions. Children can learn that all feelings are valid, but not all behaviours are. It is alright to feel angry, but it's not okay to hit or hurt.

Over the course of the early years, children need to learn that co-operation with rules and social norms ensures fairness and a turn for everyone. This helps children to develop self-regulation. It also develops their sense of 'conscience' – the conviction that you should do the right thing, not just do what you are told. Children say that they are keen to understand why particular rules and routines are needed in their settings.

Pretend play

The evidence suggests that pretend play is one of the most powerful contexts for children to develop self-regulation. In pretend play, children have to follow the 'rules' of the play and restrain their impulses for a time. For example, a child might want to be 'daddy' in the home corner. But if that role is taken, they might have to accept the role of being the baby if they are going to keep the play going with their friends. Equally, the child being 'daddy' needs to accept certain rules: they can't start pretending to drink from the baby's bottle, for example. But they might have to follow the 'rule' that once the baby is settled, they need to start preparing dinner.

Self-regulation involves feelings, behaviour and thinking. As the example above shows, you have to control your feelings, for example the impulse to play the role of 'daddy'. But you also have to focus your thoughts: you can't just do anything as 'daddy', you have to behave appropriately in playing the part based on what you know. If 'daddy' acts like the dog, it might be funny for a moment, but the play will soon break down.

Many children in the early years may 'play' by using and enjoying the different equipment they can access in self-chosen ways. But it is important that practitioners notice which children find pretend play hard. They might need to support them to join in with play. Practitioners can help by watching some pretend play with the child. They could comment on what is happening, and invite the child to think about how they could join in. Or they might set up a small group experience with small play people with just one other child, so there are not too many distractions. Then the practitioner can model the play by taking on roles with different play people and by encouraging the child to do the same. Over time, this can become more complex, adding more people and other elements to the play.

It is important for practitioners to enable children to develop their creativity and imagination in the early years. Play, especially pretend play, is central to young children's learning. For example, when children pretend that a stick is actually a horse and 'ride around' on it, they are using their imaginations to transform the object. They are also learning to follow rules which they've made up themselves. The stick is only a horse, if you ride on it using horse-like movements. As children take part in pretend play, they elaborate and extend their understanding of the world. They move from the world of 'what is' to a world of 'what might be'. A stick is in reality just a stick, after all: but it might be a horse, or a fire-fighter's hose, or a sword. That ability to think beyond concrete realities will also, in time, give children new ways of understanding the world. It will enable children to understand what life might be like for other people. That might include people who come from different cultures, places or different periods in history.

To learn effectively, children need:

- strong skills in self-regulation (thinking, behaviour and feelings)

- the ability to focus their attention by screening out distractions and focusing on a goal they wish to achieve

- be able to plan activities in sequence

- control their emotions, otherwise learning stops

These are the skills that support the process of learning. As they progress towards the end of EYFS, children also need to be taught the content of key areas of learning (like reading, writing and maths). Careful curriculum design is necessary to help practitioners teach this content in small, achievable chunks. In this way, support for *how* children learn is carefully interwoven with *what* they need to learn. The Center on the Developing Child at Harvard University comments that: 'Interventions that include an explicit focus on executive function skills do not need to be implemented separately from those focused on instruction in early literacy and math abilities. Indeed, the complex interactions that occur among executive functioning, social competence, and academic skills in preschool classrooms underscore the likely value of blending interventions designed to strengthen working memory, inhibition, and attention control with curricula focused on early literacy and math skill'.

The evidence we have about self-regulation is still limited. Few studies have assessed the educational impact, for example on early mathematics or literacy skills. However, it is important to note the significance and potential impact of practice in this area:

Improving the self-regulation skills of children in the early years

'The development of self-regulation and executive function is consistently linked with successful learning, including pre-reading skills, early mathematics and problem solving. Strategies that seek to improve learning by increasing self-regulation have an average impact of five additional months' progress. A number of studies suggest that improving the self-regulation skills of children in the early years is likely to have a lasting positive impact on later learning at school, and also have a positive impact on wider outcomes such as behaviour and persistence.'

Education Endowment Foundation: Early Years Toolkit

Find out more

The development of children's metacognition, self-regulation and executive function	<ul><li>*Building the brain's 'air traffic control' system: how early experiences shape the development of Executive Function* (Center on the Developing Child at Harvard University, 2011)</li><li>*Self-regulation snapshots* by Desiree Murray and Katie Rosanbalm (2018)</li><li>Anderson, H., Coltman, P., Page, C and Whitebread, D. (2003) 'Developing Independent Learning in Children aged 3–5'</li></ul>

PARTNERSHIP WITH PARENTS

- It is important for parents and early years settings to have a strong and respectful partnership. This sets the scene for children to thrive in the early years.

- This includes listening regularly to parents, and giving parents clear information about their children's progress.

- The help that parents give their children at home has a very significant impact on their learning.

- Some children get much less support for their learning at home than others. By knowing and understanding all the children and their families, settings can offer extra help to those who need it most.

- It's important to encourage all parents to chat, play and read with their children.

Well-qualified practitioners have expert, wide-ranging knowledge about children's development and learning. Parents have in-depth knowledge of their own children.

Both parties must come together to form a strong, co-operative and respectful partnership. That way, children can be helped through any ups and downs they may experience. A co-operative partnership can support children to become confident and curious, supporting their developing mental health and feelings of security. That will help children to thrive in the Early Years Foundation Stage, and beyond.

These types of positive partnerships can be life-changing for children and their families.

> ## We could not ask for more
>
> 'As parents we could not ask for more from a nursery. We always felt that Zuhayr was in safe hands and the fact that everyone from the leadership team, the early years practitioners to the admin and SEN staff - everyone has helped shape Zuhayr to who he has become today. He was always happy at nursery and I could see the bonds he has formed with staff members and children. Every time I mention Forest School his face lights up. I never thought I would be able to have a two way conversation with my son. It brings me the biggest joy.'
>
> Ruksana and Zahidul (Zuhayr's mum and dad)
>
> *From an email to their child's early years setting*

There is considerable research showing the importance of children's Home Learning Environment (HLE). The HLE has even more impact on children's learning than high-quality early education and care. A briefing paper from Action for Children by Rebecca Smees and Pam Sammons provides an accessible summary of the key issues.

The HLE refers to the opportunities for learning that occur in the home. This includes toys to play with, books to share, and paints, pencils and crayons to draw with. The most important learning opportunities occur through conversations and play between the child and others at home. The activities which have the strongest impact are those in the area of language and literacy. These include conversation, pretend play and shared enjoyment of books, songs and nursery rhymes.

There are many other important learning opportunities for children at home. These include developing physical skills like football, dancing or gymnastics. The important thing is that there is some kind of learning involved. This requires children to focus and to regulate their behaviour. This in turns helps their developing self-regulation. So, home learning provides many opportunities for social and emotional development.

Children who have rich learning experiences regularly at home will typically go on to achieve better in school. They will be better behaved and show more signs of emotional wellbeing. There is a lower likelihood that they will have a special educational need. These advantages carry on all the way through to the end of secondary education and into adulthood. This applies to all children with a stimulating HLE, particularly those living in disadvantage.

However, there are some important issues to be cautious about.

First, many efforts to improve HLE involve parents attending workshops or courses. But the parents who might benefit the most from these sorts of events may not attend them, or may start attending but not complete. Many barriers might stop them from participating.

So, settings will need to consider first which parents might need support. Then, they need to discuss ways of tailoring that help with parents. Parents need to feel like partners, and they need to feel motivated to engage. Settings can use the Early Years Pupil Premium to pay for this work.

Some parents may be affected by serious issues. These include alcohol or drug misuse, mental health difficulties or domestic violence. Children in extreme family environments will miss out on many of the conditions they need to thrive, including a positive HLE. It is important for settings to work positively with families in difficulty. The orderly nature of the setting can be especially important for the children. Early Years settings are also well-placed to work with other agencies. Together, they can ensure that families receive the early help or social care they need.

Overall, differences in HLE are stark, although of course there is much variability at family level. As you get to know families well, you may notice girls getting more support for learning at home than boys. You may notice that children from more affluent homes have more opportunities for learning at home. They may hear more words spoken, engage in more conversations, and have more books read to them.

So, it is vital for early years settings to work positively with parents. That way, they can help parents to improve their children's HLE. Often parents do not realise that playing, having conversations and reading with their children every day build up over time. As they understand this, they will be more likely to try out activities which will have a powerful and lasting influence on their children.

Barriers which some parents might face

Every family in unique. It's important for practitioners to get to know every child and their family, value them, and understand them.

Parents may face significant barriers which make it hard for them to focus on home learning with their child. It's important to know about those barriers, and be positive, sympathetic, and encouraging as parents make small changes.

Those barriers might include:

- Time and energy (for example, parents not having time and energy due to work outside the home, household chores and/or caring for other children)

- Knowledge, emotions and confidence (for example, parents being worried about not doing things right, or lacking confidence in their own reading and writing)

- Perceptions of responsibility (for example, parents thinking it's the nursery's or school's job to provide education and learning activities).

Sharing key information with parents

The Statutory Framework for the Early Years Foundation Stage sets out three specific reporting requirements to ensure that parents are well-informed.

1. Throughout the EYFS

At any time, if practitioners are concerned about a child's progress in any of the prime areas, they should discuss this with the child's parents. Practitioners and parents will then need to agree how they will give extra support to the child, at home and in the setting.

2. Progress check at age two

Practitioners must undertake the progress check at age two for children on roll, aged between two and three. Undertaken in collaboration with parents, this can help practitioners to discuss how well the child is progressing, and how parents might further support their child's talking, playing and learning at home

The written summary must also tell parents if there are any areas where the child's progress is less than expected.

Significant emerging concerns

Significant emerging concerns

'If there are significant emerging concerns, or an identified special educational need or disability, practitioners should develop a targeted plan to support the child's future learning and development involving parents and/or carers and other professionals (for example, the provider's Special Educational Needs Co-ordinator (SENCO) or health professionals) as appropriate.'

Statutory framework for the early years foundation stage: early adopter version

(Department for Education, 2020)

---

3. Early Years Foundation Stage Profile

In the final term of the Reception year, settings must complete the EYFS Profile for each child. The Profile should provide parents, practitioners and teachers with:

- a well-rounded picture of a child's knowledge, understanding and abilities

- their attainment against expected levels

- information about the child's readiness for Year 1

The Profile must reflect practitioners' own knowledge and professional judgement of a child. This will inform discussions with parents and carers, and any other adults whom the teacher, parent or carer judges can offer a useful contribution.

The Profile is a quick check of a child's learning at the end of the EYFS. There is no need for practitioners to begin 'tracking' children's progress against the profile from the start of the Reception year. Instead, the profile should be completed briskly and accurately during the summer term. Its purpose is to support transition, promote dialogue with parents, identify possible barriers to learning, and inform teaching in Year 1.

It's important to listen regularly to parents, and give them clear information about the progress their children are making. Parents also need to know if their children are having difficulties, and how they can work with practitioners to help children through any such difficulties.

Parents are a source of rich and essential information about their children's learning and wellbeing. This is crucial when children first come into a setting. It remains important throughout their time there.

Working with parents and supporting children's learning at home	**Find out more**
	• *Improving the home learning environment: a behaviour change approach* (H.M Government and the National Literacy Trust, 2018)
	• *Working with parents to support children's learning* (Education Endowment Foundation, 2018)
	• *Effects of the Home Learning Environment and Preschool Center Experience upon Literacy and Numeracy Development in Early Primary School* (2008) by Melhuish, E., Phan, M., Sylva, K., Sammons, P., Siraj-Blatchford, I. and Taggart, B.
	• 'Hungry Little Minds: Simple, fun activities for kids, from newborn to five' (online)
	• 'Making it REAL' is an award-winning programme that works with practitioners to support children's early literacy and development.

IMPROVING THIS GUIDANCE

We hope that you have enjoyed reading this document and that it supports you as you develop your practice. But like everything else we do in the early years to keep improving, this can only be work in progress and never the 'final word'.

We'd love to hear back from you. What do you like about the guidance? What could be better?

We'd especially like to hear from you if you'd like to help us to improve this document. If your contribution is published, we'll acknowledge your authorship and send you a free copy of the next edition.

You can give your feedback and suggestions by clicking on the feedback link on our website, www.development-matters.org.uk

No-one was paid to write this document. We think we're better when we all work together to improve things for children and practitioners in the early years. This document has been published at the lowest possible price to cover all costs. If we make a small profit, that will go straight back into improving the services we offer for children and their families at Sheringham Nursery School and Children's Centre.

The team at Sheringham Nursery School and Children's Centre

ABOUT DEVELOPMENT MATTERS

Development Matters was commissioned by the Department for Education as non-statutory guidance to support practitioners in delivering the revised Early Years Foundation Stage (EYFS) from 2021, and to support early adopter schools in 2020.

The guidance builds on the 2012 version, and also draws on the original *Curriculum Guidance for the Early Years Foundation Stage (2000)* and *Birth to Three Matters* (2003). The Communication section draws on the work of I CAN. The Expressive Arts and Design section draws on the work of Nicola Burke's *Musical Development Matters*.

Development Matters is the latest in the line of high-quality, research-informed and non-statutory guidance. It was written to support the many dedicated early years practitioners who in turn support the learning and development of our youngest children.

Almost 15 years on since the introduction of the Early Years Foundation Stage, it builds on many excellent documents which have informed practice across a range of settings and supporting the diverse needs of children. A selective list, which is far from exhaustive, includes:

- The EPPSE Project
- The SEED Project
- The FEEL Study
- The Inclusive Classroom Profile
- The Early Years Learning and Development Literature Review
- The EEF Early Years Toolkit
- Practitioners' experiences of the Early Years Foundation Stage
- Children's Experiences of the Early Years Foundation Stage
- Playing, learning and interacting

We would also like to acknowledge the work of the Centre for Inclusive Practice at the UCL Institute of Education, and the work of Professor Lynn Ang and Dr Sinéad Harmey to support the Manor Park Talks programme on early communication.

There has been lots done, but as ever, there remains lots more to do. Further constructive critique, conversation and collaboration are the only ways we will strengthen our ability to support the early education, care and development of our youngest children.

Many people worked to develop *Development Matters* including:

The EYFS Advisory Panel	
Clare Sealy	St Matthias School
Julian Grenier	Sheringham Nursery School and Children's Centre
Dame Alison Peacock	Chartered College of Teaching
Emma Lennard	Civitas
Gill Jones HMI	Ofsted
James Bowen	National Association of Headteachers
Sara-Jayne Martin	Roxbourne Primary School
Sir Kevan Collins	Education Endowment Foundation
Beatrice Merrick	Early Education
Iram Siraj	Oxford University
Jan Dubiel	Early Years Consultant

Around 200 practitioners provided feedback online and through focus group discussions. They were contacted via the Early Years Alliance, the National Association of Day Nurseries, the Teaching School Council, PACEY, local authority officers and multi-academy trust officers.

Expert advice was provided by practitioners with the following roles:

Early Help Lead

Health visitor

Developmental psychologist

Child psychotherapist

Professor of education

Communication Champion

Child Health expert

Speech and Language Therapist

Inclusion expert

Physical development and movement expert

Early Years Consultant

Early maths expert

Early education researcher

Early years policy researcher

Communication researcher

Children's Centre lead

Private nursery manager

Preschool manager

Childminder

Local authority officer

Multi-academy trust officer

Her Majesty's Inspector (Ofsted)

Nursery School headteacher

Primary school early years lead

Primary School headteacher

Local Authority Consultant

Teaching School lead for the early years

Equalities expert

Research School lead

APPENDIX 1

ASSESSMENT BEYOND LEVELS IN THE EARLY YEARS: IMPROVING LEARNING FOR ALL CHILDREN

I wrote this blog in September 2020, after a series of discussions with teachers and practitioners in some of the Early Adopter schools. Like most blogs this was written and posted at speed. As it generated a lot of discussion and interest, I decided to include it in this book

The DFE published the revised Development Matters in September 2020 so that the sector has a full year to get used to the new document before the changes to the EYFS Statutory Framework come into effect in September 2021.

This blog looks at two important areas of change: the focus on the curriculum, and changes to guidance around assessment. The purpose of the blog is twofold. Firstly, to support those schools who are early adopters of the revised EYFS Statutory Framework. Secondly, the blog aims to prompt dialogue and discussion across the sector on these important issues. But, unless you're an early adopter, it's best to stick to your existing approaches during the year ahead.

There is no need to make changes now. It is much better to implement changes in a careful, measured and unhurried way.

Early years assessment

Feedback from across the sector, and especially the findings of the Early Years Alliance report *Minds Matter*, tell us that there is a real problem around the workload involved in gathering 'evidence' of children's learning, and creating and inputting tracking 'data'.

But the problem with many current approaches goes well beyond the serious issues of workload and stress.

For many of us, the EYFS has become all about ensuring that children 'cover' everything in Development Matters and progress regularly from one age band to the next. As a headteacher, I take my share of responsibility for this situation.

We got ourselves into a way of working which was something like this:

- Assess all children on entry, using the age bands – often broken down into 'emerging' and 'secure'. So a child might be assessed overall as '30-50 emerging' on entry to a nursery at three years old.

- Plan in the next steps of learning needed to move them from '30-50 emerging' and onto '30-50 secure'

- As the weeks roll on, look at the evidence collected about the child's learning and make sure any gaps are filled. So if there is no evidence for some of the statements in Understanding the World in the 30-50 month band, the child will be encouraged into activities so that evidence can be recorded and gaps filled.

- Over time, practitioners are held accountable for progress. It is expected that the children they are responsible for will move up the bands.

- Reception teachers in particular are held accountable for checking that children are 'on track' to achieve a Good Level of Development. Sometimes they are given targets e.g. 70% to achieve a GLD.

- Where children might have a special educational need or disability, requests for extra help or funding are often be supported by assessments using Development Matters with summative comments like 'Maisie is four-years old, but she is working at the level typically expected of a child aged 8-20 months.

What's wrong with this way of working?

First, it's important to recognise the great efforts that practitioners have always made to make sure that every child gets a high-quality, rich and stimulating experience in the early years. The approaches outlined above were motivated largely be a desire to make sure that individual children, or groups of children, didn't get 'left behind'. We wanted to make sure everyone made progress.

So it's not as simple as saying there is something 'wrong' with this.

But there have been serious drawbacks with this approach.

It has been very time-consuming, and as a result all this work around assessment has taken practitioners away from what we do best: playing with children, having conversations, and helping them to learn new things.

When we're with the children, we have often put a lot of focus on making sure they are progressing up through the age-bands, or covering bullet points in *Development Matters*. We have wanted 'evidence' that children's play or activity exemplifies a particular bullet point in a particular age-band.

That's taken over from a more important aim: ensuring that children have secure understanding, before we start introducing them to new activities or ideas. I think it's well understood that a big part of our role is to make sure that children have strong foundations in their early learning and development. But we've been taken away from that by the focus on age-bands, levels and data.

Here is a brief, practical example. In the 2012 *Development Matters* the 22-36 month band in Number says 'recites some number names in sequence'. Next, the 30-50 month band says 'recites numbers in order to 10'.

That might lead a practitioner to notice that a three-year old is saying '1-2-3' and so plan, as a 'next step', that the child should be able to recite numbers in order to 10.

Once we have the 'evidence' of the child reciting from 1 to 10, we move onto the next bullet point in *Development Matters*.

The problem is that learning to count is much trickier than that. You need to be able to recite the counting sequence. You also need to be able to match one number name to one object. You need to know that the last number you say, represents the full number of the set. Children need to have many opportunities to repeat and practise this and they are likely to find it extremely difficult at first to keep all of those things in mind. That's why we see children being careful to match 1:1 and at the same time getting the number order mixed up. They are struggling to remember and act on everything they know at the same time. They need plenty of time and practice. They don't need to be rushed onto bigger numbers.

What does this mean in practice?

So if that particular approach to assessment and planning is unhelpful, what might we be doing instead?

In this blog, I am arguing that we need to switch our main focus away from tracking, assessment data, and levels. Instead, we need to focus on designing a curriculum for the children we are working with, which has a 'progress model'.

We're not very used to talking about curriculum in the early years any more, so I am aware this may seem like a daunting aim. But it actually makes a lot of sense when you think about it practically – and it takes us back to the starting point of the Early Years Foundation Stage, which is the 2000 document Curriculum Guidance for the Foundation Stage. Somehow, that focus on 'curriculum' got went missing in action over the last 20 years. I wrote about this earlier, in a piece for Impact (the journal of the Chartered College of Teachers).

Here are a few practical examples. You might decide that one goal in your nursery curriculum is for all children to be able to make a cake independently. To achieve that goal, children will need to be able to do lots of things which include (this is not an exhaustive list):

- Having the physical strength and dexterity to mix ingredients using a wooden spoon

- Ability to count accurately (e.g. 2 eggs)

- Ability to measure liquid and solid ingredients accurately

- Ability to follow a sequence (a recipe card which illustrates each step in pictures, for example)

Children will need plenty of experience and adult help along the way to get to the point where they can make that cake independently.

Likewise, you might have a goal that all children will learn to ride a two-wheeled bike by the end of the reception year. So, you might start with simple push-along wheeled toys for your two-year olds. Children might graduate from these, onto a small trike when they are ready. After they have plenty of practice (and fun!) on the trikes, they might be confident enough with their balance, pedalling and steering to ride a two-wheeled balance bike with no pedals. After some months of wobbling around, they'll soon be quickly negotiating the outdoor space and picking up speed because they can scoot with both feet, then balance with their feet off the ground. Then, they will be ready for a two-wheeled pedal bike without stabilisers. They already know about balance and pedalling; but they will need plenty of time to combine those skills together and pedal off happily on a bike.

This is what I mean by the curriculum being a progress model.

Some children will need a lot more help and scaffolding to access that curriculum. That's always been a huge strength of early years practitioners. We notice what children can, and can't do. We're good at deciding when it will be helpful to step in and support, and when it's best to be encouraging but hang back. We know that some children will learn something tricky like using scissors by watching, copying others, and trial and error; and others will need some focused direct instruction about which fingers to put in the two holes, etc.

Once you have that 'big picture' curriculum, it makes sense to focus assessment on the key milestones on the way to those curricular goals. So, instead of focusing on the age bands in Development Matters, you might be focussing on when a child moves from trike to bike. If a child is a skilled trike rider, you might need to encourage that move – it may not happen naturally. Accurate assessment helps us know when to step in and encourage the child onto the next milestone in the curriculum we have set out.

So, it's advisable to make the focus of your assessment something clear and specific that a child needs to be able to do, or needs to know. In turn, that means practitioners need to understand how the different elements of the curriculum fit together to help children build their learning over time.

We also need to have a secure understanding of child development. We need to understand the features of effective pedagogy: judging when to get involved and when to encourage; knowing how to scaffold children's learning so we support them to keep trying without over-helping them. This is, frankly, going to be a big challenge for us – whilst a great many early years practitioners have that secure understanding of child development and pedagogy, others haven't. They may, for example, have been let down in their initial training. Leaders and managers need to prioritise high-quality, sustained professional development for our team. We need to have in-depth professional knowledge as well as practical experience and passion.

It's important to be sensible about not going too far with the curriculum model. If a group of children have just found hundreds of woodlice teeming under a log, it will be time to get down with them to observe the woodlice. We will be getting the magnifying glasses, encouraging children to talk about their ideas, and linking what they are seeing to books or videos on YouTube. Plans must be flexible, and go with children's fascinations and interests.

In summary, we need to create a curriculum for our children which is built on a progress model. We need to focus our assessment on the key milestones in that model. We need to be sure that children are secure in what they know and can do, before introducing them to something new. You wouldn't expect children to follow a recipe sequence card if they've never measured anything in a jug, or if they can't accurately count the number of eggs shown.

Following children's interests

At this point, you may be saying – isn't it better to help young children by following their interests? Can't we teach them everything they need to know by extending on their play?

The brief answer is that encouraging children's self-chosen play is, indeed, really important. Children learn a huge amount through the play they choose. We can help maximise that by making sure we provide a high-quality learning environment. Sometimes, we might sensitively get involved and extend their play. For that to work, I would argue that we need a systematic approach to evaluating the quality of that environment, and those interactions, so that we can build on what we do well, and improve where we need to. An example of that approach is the suite of *Curriculum, Leadership and Interaction Quality Rating Scales (CLIQRS): the UK family of rating scales* published by the UCL-IOE Press, and the *ITERS-3* and *ECERS-3* scales.

Play is central in the EYFS. Nothing in this blog is intended to question that.

But children can't learn everything they need, to get that secure foundation in their early learning, unless the adults also offer guided experiences and engaging teaching sessions with clear learning intentions as well as supporting their play.

This is explained neatly in a 2018 paper called 'Myths of Early Math' by the American researchers Douglas Clements and Julie Sarama. Here are two of the myths. You can follow up the evidence for each of their claims by clicking on the links.

6. "Math Centers Are All You Need."

Fact. Math learning centers, such as a table with a variety of manipulatives or a building blocks center, if well designed and supervised, probably contribute to children's mathematics experiences.

Myth. Centers are insufficient by themselves. At no age level is it recommended that education should be entirely "child-centered" *or* "teacher-directed". Interaction with adults is key in all domains and activities in small groups appear particularly effective. However, mathematics, more so than other content areas, *builds*— concepts and skills are connected, abstracted, and curtailed, and become the object of thinking at a new level of mathematical thought. Centers, as usually implemented, promote incidental learning at best and rarely build one mathematical idea on the next. Finally, only intentional activities focused on mathematics appear to make significant contributions to children's learning.

7. "The Best Way to Teach Math is through "Teachable Moments."

Fact. Teachable moments, handled well, can be wondrous and satisfying.

Myth. However, teachable moments alone are far from adequate. The teacher must carefully observe children and identify elements in the spontaneously-emerging situations that can be used to promote learning of mathematics. However, there are serious problems with depending solely on this approach. For example, most teachers spend little time on careful observation necessary to find such moments, and spend little time with children during their free play. Most teachers have a difficult time engaging children in tasks at their mathematical level. Most teachers do not have applicable mathematics language and concepts at the ready, such as *relational* terms in mathematics. Finally, even if professional development could address all of these issues, it is unrealistic for any teacher to see opportunities for multiple children to build multiple concepts consistently over the year.

That's why the diagram at the start of the 2012 version of *Development Matters* is both helpful, and limited:

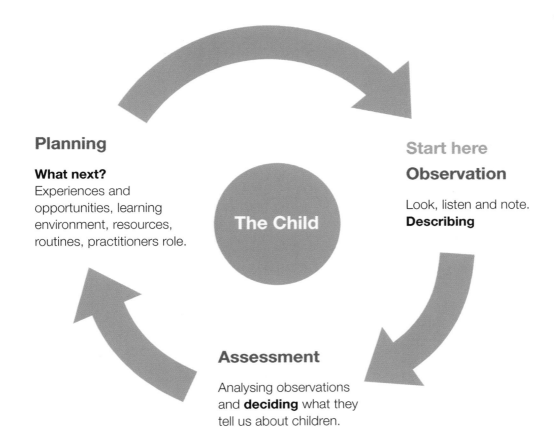

Planning

What next?
Experiences and opportunities, learning environment, resources, routines, practitioners role.

The Child

Start here
Observation

Look, listen and note.
Describing

Assessment

Analysing observations and **deciding** what they tell us about children.

The diagram is helpful because it's so important that we observe carefully what children can do, and then build on that. If we aren't clear what children know and can do, we can't be much help to them.

But it's unhelpful, because it misses out the 'big picture' of what we want children to learn. If we always 'start here' observing the child, we might do a good job of noticing and building on their interests. But what about things they have never seen, or done, or been part of? If we never see a child taking part in maths-rich play, we need to make sure we introduce them to those important concepts about shapes and patterns (for example). Otherwise, some children will miss out. Often, the children that miss out are those who are disadvantaged or vulnerable in other ways.

The updated *Development Matters* encourages practitioners and settings to develop a curriculum which is both appropriate for the children in their care, and is ambitious. That's why it's a shorter document (the 2020 version is around two thirds of the length of the 2012 version). With less guidance, there is more freedom to do what's right for the children we're working with.

Development Matters exists to support practitioners and settings as we develop that curriculum. It helps us to reflect on whether the curriculum we are designing is broad enough, and to check that we're building in a progress model. For babies and toddlers, that notion of 'curriculum' should be pretty light-touch. We might consider the key experiences we want babies and toddlers to be introduced to, like Treasure Basket and Heuristic Play. There may be particular outdoor experiences on our curriculum map, too, and a range of songs, rhymes and books. These are just some examples, not a comprehensive list. I also think it's important to think of Development Matters as the floor, not the ceiling. We don't want children to experience anything less than what's suggested; but we also don't want adherence to the guidance to cap our expectations or limit what we think children can do.

It is especially important to note that the Early Learning Goals are not the curriculum for the reception year. They are just 17 checkpoints to help us summarise what a child knows and can do, and where they might need more help. If the whole effort of the reception year is focussed on the goals, then children will experience a very narrow curriculum. If vulnerable children miss out on a rich early years curriculum in reception, who else will provide it?

A rush towards the goals also risks depriving children of the foundational attitudes, skills, knowledge and confidence they need to be successful learners throughout their schooling. It's meaningless to say that a child has a 'good level of development' if in reality they have just been coaxed through 17 hoops. We end up with positive data, and with children who haven't received the sort of curriculum they were entitled to, and who are not ready for Key Stage One either.

Feedback is important

The observation-assessment-planning diagram from the 2012 *Development Matters* can also be usefully extended by thinking about the importance of feedback and scaffolding.

Whilst some observations are written down, analysed, and acted on in planning, there is a second, more powerful and more immediate cycle. That's when practitioners notice something about what a child is doing, or saying, and they give the child helpful feedback there and then. They might point something out: 'I think that block there is a bit wonky, perhaps that's why your tower is shaking?' Or they might encourage a child to notice something whilst they draw: 'can you see that the petals aren't quite that colour? You've done a really good job, but maybe it's worth another try at mixing the paints?'

Helping children to reflect on their learning and to refine key skills is much more important than writing things down and giving them a level. By showing our confidence that they can keep getting better when they try hard and persevere, we reinforce the important idea that we don't have 'fixed' abilities. We can all get better at what we do if we get the right support, encouragement, and help. Effort matters.

Measuring progress from children's starting points

We need to think differently about children's progress. We need to get away from over-complicated systems which tie up too much of our time, baffle parents, and don't help children.

On the other hand, we need approaches which can be used sensibly and help us focus on what children need.

Here is an example of how children's development might be assessed on entry to Reception. This is a suggestion only – it's not meant to be prescriptive, and it's clear that the responsibility for both the design of the curriculum and the assessment alongside it sits with schools and settings.

On entry to Reception, the main focus of the teacher and early years educator will be to settle the child into this new, exciting and demanding place they're in: 'big school'.

Checking children's development in the prime areas of the EYFS will undoubtedly be useful – both to help them as they settle, and to give an indication of their starting points.

So that could involve:

- **Noticing how the child communicates. Are they saying mainly one or two-word statements, or speaking in sentences? Can you generally understand what they say? What languages do they speak? Do they appear to understand what you say to them?** A few telling examples will cover this. Note down the exact words they spoke whilst they played with you. Find out more from their parents.

- **Observing the child's confidence. Do they get stuck in and start to play from day one? Are they sociable and quick to make friends? Or do they struggle to separate from their parent?** Again, a few telling examples will cover all you need. What happened the first time when their parent left? Is there an example of them playing with another child? What do parents say?

- **Noticing the child's physical competence and also their self-care. This will include how they manage hand-washing and toileting, snack and mealtimes. How do they manage steps and equipment for large motor skill development like slides? How do they manage equipment for small motor skill development like construction kits or colouring pencils?** Once again, teachers and early years educators will quickly get a sense of the child's development in this area, which can usefully be supplemented by parents.

These assessments will inform an early discussion with parents about how well their child is settling, and if any extra help is needed.

There isn't any need to turn these assessments into levels with numbers attached. It is also important to bear in mind that things change quickly for young children: the child who seems very shy and withdrawn in September might really 'come out of their shell' later in the term, once they are used to coming into school.

Based on this information, teachers can quickly identify which children are starting at a level which means they're ready to take part in the reception curriculum, and which children are struggling to start school and join in with the other children and the activities because of difficulties in one or more areas like communication, understanding, confidence and self-care.

Those 'vulnerable starters' will quickly need extra help. It will be important to get to know and understand them. What are their interests? What exactly do they find hard? How can their parents best offer them extra help? Is there important information from their previous setting or from their health visitor to take into account? (By the way, I am sure someone can think of a better term than 'vulnerable starters').

For the majority of children, the assessments above will give starting points which it's simple to show progress from. Maybe they were speaking in a simple sentence, like 'I want lego' in September. By November, in story sessions where you are encouraging the children to comment on the story and give their own ideas, you might notice a child say 'the caterpillar ate the leaf because he had a bellyache'. The progress model in the curriculum (introducing dialogic story sessions) supports the child to speak in more complex sentences. As they access the curriculum, they make progress.

There are a few important issues to bear in mind about these starting points:

Children in the 'vulnerable starters' group need lots of support in their early days in Reception. For example, if their language is a concern, the main support you will give is extra attention when they are playing to encourage conversations. You might also use an evidence-based intervention like the Nuffield Early Language Intervention (NELI). It's important to give the children the help they need quickly.

1. Those 'starting points' are not anchors. Many children with low starting points will do really well in their reception year – they just got off to a shaky start. It's important to offer the children the scaffolding and support they need so that they can access the whole rich and stimulating curriculum that's on offer. Otherwise, a ceiling will be placed on their potential. Assessment and curriculum design should be ambitious and inclusive.

2. It is not true to say that children with SEND are learning 'like younger children'. It does not make sense to give them a level like '16-26 months'. Instead, precise assessment needs to focus on what the child can do, and what the barriers to their learning are. If a child has specific difficulties with their communication, for example, they may need to have aids like a core vocabulary board so that they can make choices and share their ideas. All children are entitled to the whole of the early years curriculum. Of course, they won't all manage to do and know everything that's mapped out: but some who appear vulnerable at first may thrive later in the year. So it is important that levels and grouping do not become self-fulfilling prophecies that hold children back. It's important that we focus on support, scaffolding, and helping children to overcome barriers to their learning.

3. It makes sense to focus on progress from starting points through a well-designed curriculum. A summer born child, or a more vulnerable starter, will benefit hugely if they can make secure, steady, step-by-step progress so that they can access a broad curriculum in the early years and key stage one. Looking at the medium-to-long term like this is much more helpful than racing to get a child to a Good Level of Development' regardless of how secure their learning is.

4. When the Early Learning Goals become a 'high stakes' accountability measure, they become an inaccurate measure of a child's readiness for year 1. In turn, that stops them from being a useful way to reflect on the quality and impact of the early years curriculum.

My final point is this: let's remember why we all went into working in the early years.

We're here because we want to give every child a great first experience of playing and learning outside their home. We want to play our part in giving them the best possible start to their learning.

Should we be putting so much effort into creating masses of unhelpful tracking data about children? I'm arguing that that it's time to stop that. Instead, let's put our efforts into improving learning for all children.

APPENDIX 2

DEVELOPMENT MATTERS

INTRODUCTION

No job is more important than working with children in the early years.

Development Matters has been written for all early years practitioners, for childminders and staff in nurseries, nursery schools, and nursery and reception classes in school. It offers a top-level view of how children develop and learn. It guides, but does not replace, professional judgement.

The guidance can also help you to meet the requirements of the *statutory framework for the early years foundation stage*. The framework sets out the three prime areas of learning that underpin everything in the early years:

- communication and language

- physical development

- personal, social and emotional development

- The four specific areas help children to strengthen and apply the prime areas:

- literacy

- mathematics

- understanding the world

- expressive arts and design

All of those areas of learning are connected together. The characteristics of effective teaching and learning weave through them all. That's because children in the early years are becoming more powerful learners and thinkers. These characteristics develop as they learn to do new things, acquire new skills, develop socially and emotionally, and become better communicators.

Development Matters sets out the pathways of children's development in broad ages and stages. However, the actual learning of young children is not so neat and orderly. The main purpose of these pathways is therefore to help you assess each child's level of development. Accurate assessment helps practitioners to make informed decisions about what a child needs to learn and be able to do next.

The document is not a tick list for generating lots of data. You can use your professional knowledge to help children make progress without needing to record lots of next steps. Settings can help children to make progress without generating unnecessary paperwork.

Examples of effective practice mentioned early on are often relevant for older children. For example, the communication and language section says that 'babies and toddlers thrive when you show a genuine interest in them, join in and respond warmly.'

Of course, this is also true for children of all ages.

The guidance can help you check that children are secure in all the earlier steps of learning before you look at their 'age band'. Depth in learning matters much more than moving from one band to the next or trying to cover everything. A child's learning is secure if they show it consistently and in a range of different contexts.

For example, it is important to give a child many opportunities to deepen their understanding of numbers up to five. There is no value in rushing to 10.

The observation checkpoints can help you to notice whether a child is at risk of falling behind in their development. You can make all the difference by taking action quickly, using your professional judgement and your understanding of child development. By monitoring the child's progress more closely, you can make the right decisions about what sort of extra help is needed. Through sensitive dialogue with parents ('parent' is used throughout this document to refer to parents, carers and guardians), you can begin to understand the child better and also offer helpful suggestions to support the home learning environment.

When children are at earlier stages of development than expected, it is important to notice what they enjoy doing and also find out where their difficulties may lie. They need extra help so that they become secure in the earlier stages of development. It is not helpful to wait for them to become 'ready'. For example, children who are not speaking in sentences are not going to be able to write in sentences. They will need lots of stimulating experiences to help them develop their communication. That's why the time you spend listening to them and having conversations with them is so important.

Health colleagues, like health visitors or speech and language therapists, offer vital extra support to this work.

It is vital that we get to know and value all young children. All children learn more in the period from birth to five years old than any other time in their lives. If children are at risk of falling behind the majority, the best time to help them to catch up and keep up is in the early years. Every child can make progress, if they are given the right support.

When we succeed in giving every child the best start in their early years, we give them what they need today. We also set them up with every chance of success tomorrow.

Seven Features of Effective Practice

1 The best for every child

- All children deserve to have an equal chance of success.

- High-quality early education is good for all children. It is especially important for children from disadvantaged backgrounds.

- When they start school, children from disadvantaged backgrounds are, on average, 4 months behind their peers. We need to do more to narrow that gap.

- Children who have lived through difficult experiences can begin to grow stronger when they experience high quality early education and care.

- High-quality early education and care is inclusive. Children's special educational needs and disabilities (SEND) are identified quickly. All children promptly receive any extra help they need, so they can progress well in their learning.

2 High-quality care

- The child's experience must always be central to the thinking of every practitioner.

- Babies, toddlers and young children thrive when they are loved and well cared for.

- High-quality care is consistent. Every practitioner needs to enjoy spending time with young children.

- Effective practitioners are responsive to children and babies. They notice when a baby looks towards them and gurgles and respond with pleasure.

- Practitioners understand that toddlers are learning to be independent, so they will sometimes get frustrated.

- Practitioners know that starting school, and all the other transitions in the early years, are big steps for small children.

3 The curriculum: what we want children to learn

- The curriculum is a top-level plan of everything the early years setting wants the children to learn.

- Planning to help every child to develop their language is vital.

- The curriculum needs to be ambitious. Careful sequencing will help children to build their learning over time.

- Young children's learning is often driven by their interests. Plans need to be flexible.

- Babies and young children do not develop in a fixed way. Their development is like a spider's web with many strands, not a straight line.

- Depth in early learning is much more important than covering lots of things in a superficial way.

4 Pedagogy: helping children to learn

- Children are powerful learners. Every child can make progress in their learning, with the right help.
- Effective pedagogy is a mix of different approaches. Children learn through play, by adults modelling, by observing each other, and through guided learning and direct teaching.

- Practitioners carefully organise enabling environments for high-quality play. Sometimes, they make time and space available for children to invent their own play. Sometimes, they join in to sensitively support and extend children's learning.
- Children in the early years also learn through group work, when practitioners guide their learning.
- Older children need more of this guided learning.
- A well-planned learning environment, indoors and outside, is an important aspect of pedagogy.

5 Assessment: checking what children have learnt

- Assessment is about noticing what children can do and what they know. It is not about lots of data and evidence.

- Effective assessment requires practitioners to understand child development. Practitioners also need to be clear about what they want children to know and be able to do.

- Accurate assessment can highlight whether a child has a special educational need and needs extra help.
- Before assessing children, it's a good idea to think about whether the assessments will be useful.
- Assessment should not take practitioners away from the children for long periods of time.

6 Self-regulation and executive function

- Executive function includes the child's ability to:
  - hold information in mind
  - focus their attention
  - regulate their behaviour
  - plan what to do next.

- These abilities contribute to the child's growing ability to self-regulate:
  - focus their thinking
  - monitor what they are doing and adapt
  - regulate strong feelings
  - be patient for what they want
  - bounce back when things get difficult.
- Language development is central to self-regulation: children use language to guide their actions and plans. Pretend play gives many opportunities for children to focus their thinking, persist and plan ahead.

7 Partnership with parents

- It is important for parents and early years settings to have a strong and respectful partnership. This sets the scene for children to thrive in the early years.
- This includes listening regularly to parents and giving parents clear information about their children's progress.

- The help that parents give their children at home has a very significant impact on their learning.
- Some children get much less support for their learning at home than others. By knowing and understanding all the children and their families, settings can offer extra help to those who need it most.

- It is important to encourage all parents to chat, play and read with their children.

The characteristics of effective teaching and learning

In planning and guiding what children learn, practitioners must reflect on the different rates at which children are developing and adjust their practice appropriately. Three characteristics of effective teaching and learning are:

- playing and exploring – children investigate and experience things, and 'have a go'

- active learning – children concentrate and keep on trying if they encounter difficulties, and enjoy achievements

- creating and thinking critically – children have and develop their own ideas, make links between ideas, and develop strategies for doing things

Statutory framework for the early years foundation stage: early adopter version

Playing and exploring

Children will be learning to:	Examples of how to support this:
Realise that their actions have an effect on the world, so they want to keep repeating them.	Encourage babies' exploration of the world around them. Suggestions: investigating the feel of their key person's hair or reaching for a blanket in their cot. Play games like 'Peepo'. As they get more familiar, the baby or toddler will increasingly lead the play and want the adult to respond.
Reach for and accept objects. Make choices and explore different resources and materials.	Show and give babies interesting things, such as a rattle or a soft toy. Arrange for babies to take part in Treasure Basket play. Offer open-ended resources for babies and toddlers to play freely with, outdoors and inside.
Plan and think ahead about how they will explore or play with objects.	Provide different pebbles, shells and other natural materials for children to explore and arrange freely.
Guide their own thinking and actions by talking to themselves while playing. For example, a child doing a jigsaw might whisper under their breath: "Where does that one go? — I need to find the big horse next." 	Help children to develop more control over their actions by giving them many opportunities to play freely and find their own ways of solving problems. When appropriate, sensitively provide a helpful commentary. You might suggest: "Why don't you look for the biggest pieces first?" That will help a child who is trying to solve a jigsaw. Children may copy your commentary by talking out loud to themselves first. In time, this will develop into their 'inner voice'.

Children will be learning to:	Examples of how to support this:
Make independent choices. Do things independently that they have been previously taught.	Provide a well-organised environment so that children know where materials and tools are and can access them easily. Provide enough materials and arrange spaces so that children can collaborate and learn alongside peers. Once children know how to use scissors, they can use this skill to achieve what they want to do. For example, they may want to make a mask or cut out material for a collage.
Bring their own interests and fascinations into early years settings. This helps them to develop their learning.	Extend children's interests by providing stimulating resources for them to play with, on their own and with peers, in response to their fascinations. Join in with children's play and investigations, without taking over. Talk with them about what they are doing and what they are noticing. Provide appropriate non-fiction books and links to information online to help them follow their interests.
Respond to new experiences that you bring to their attention.	Regularly provide new materials and interesting things for children to explore and investigate. Introduce children to different styles of music and art. Give them the opportunity to observe changes in living things in the setting, and around the local environment. Take children to new places, like a local theatre or museum.

Active learning

Children will be learning to:	Examples of how to support this:
Participate in routines, such as going to their cot or mat when they want to sleep. Begin to predict sequences because they know routines. For example, they may anticipate lunch when they see the table being set, or get their coat when the door to the outdoor area opens.	Help babies, toddlers and young children feel safe, secure and treasured as individuals. The key person approach gives children a secure base of care and affection, together with supportive routines. That can help them to explore and play confidently.
Show goal-directed behaviour. For example, babies may pull themselves up by using the edges of a low table to reach for a toy on top of the table. Toddlers might turn a storage box upside down so they can stand on it and reach up for an object.	Provide furniture and boxes at the right height to encourage babies to pull themselves up and reach for objects. Opportunities to play and explore freely, indoors and outside, are fun. They also help babies, toddlers and young children to develop their self-regulation as they enjoy hands-on learning and sometimes talk about what they are doing.
Use a range of strategies to reach a goal they have set themselves.	Provide plenty of high-quality, open-ended resources for children to play with freely, inside and outdoors. Suggestion: children can use wooden blocks to make lots of different structures.
Begin to correct their mistakes themselves. For example, instead of using increasing force to push a puzzle piece into the slot, they try another piece to see if it will fit.	Help young children to develop by accepting the pace of their learning. Give them plenty of time to make connections and repeat activities.
Keep on trying when things are difficult.	Help children to think about what will support them most, taking care not to offer help too soon. Some children learn by repeating something hard on their own. They learn through trial and error. Others learn by asking a friend or an adult for help. Others learn by modelling. They watch what you do or what other children do.

Creating and thinking critically

Children will be learning to	Examples of how to support this:
Take part in simple pretend play. For example, they might use an object like a brush to pretend to brush their hair, or 'drink' from a pretend cup. Sort materials. For example, at tidy-up time, children know how to put different construction materials in separate baskets.	Help babies, toddlers and young children to find their own ideas by providing open-ended resources that can be used in many different ways. Encourage and enjoy children's creative thinking as they find new ways to do things. Children need consistent routines and plenty of time so that play is not constantly interrupted. It is important to be reflective and flexible.
Review their progress as they try to achieve a goal. Check how well they are doing. Solve real problems: for example, to share nine strawberries between three friends, they might put one in front of each, then a second, and finally a third. Finally, they might check at the end that everyone has the same number of strawberries.	Help children to reflect on and talk about their learning through using photographs and learning journeys. Share in children's pride about their achievements and their enjoyment of special memories. Suggestion: you could prompt a conversation with questions like: "Do you remember when…?", "How would you would do that now?" or "I wonder what you were thinking then?"
Use pretend play to think beyond the 'here and now' and to understand another perspective. For example, a child role-playing the billy goats gruff might suggest that "Maybe the troll is lonely and hungry? That's why he is fierce."	Help children to extend their ideas through sustained discussion that goes beyond what they, and you, have noticed. Consider 'how' and 'why' things happen.

Children will be learning to	Examples of how to support this:
Know more, so feel confident about coming up with their own ideas. Make more links between those ideas.	Help children to look come up with their own ideas and explanations. Suggestion: you could look together at woodlice outdoors with the magnifying app on a tablet. You could ask: "What's similar about woodlice and other insects?" You could use and explain terms like 'antennae' and 'thorax'.
Concentrate on achieving something that's important to them. They are increasingly able to control their attention and ignore distractions.	Offer children many different experiences and opportunities to play freely and to explore and investigate. Make time and space for children to become deeply involved in imaginative play, indoors and outside.

Communication and language

The development of children's spoken language underpins all seven areas of learning and development. Children's back-and-forth interactions from an early age form the foundations for language and cognitive development. The number and quality of the conversations they have with adults and peers throughout the day in a language-rich environment is crucial. By commenting on what children are interested in or doing, and echoing back what they say with new vocabulary added, practitioners will build children's language effectively. Reading frequently to children, and engaging them actively in stories, non-fiction, rhymes and poems, and then providing them with extensive opportunities to use and embed new words in a range of contexts, will give children the opportunity to thrive. Through conversation, story-telling and role play, where children share their ideas with support and modelling from their teacher, and sensitive questioning that invites them to elaborate, children become comfortable using a rich range of vocabulary and language structures.

Statutory framework for the early years foundation stage: early adopter version

English as an additional language

Speaking more than one language has lots of advantages for children. It is the norm in many countries around the world. Children will learn English from a strong foundation in their home language. It is important for you to encourage families to use their home language for linguistic as well as cultural reasons. Children learning English will typically go through a quiet phase when they do not say very much and may then use words in both languages in the same sentence. Talk to parents about what language they speak at home, try and learn a few key words and celebrate multilingualism in your setting.

Babies, toddlers and young children will be learning to:	Examples of how to support this:
Turn towards familiar sounds. They are also startled by loud noises and accurately locate the source of a familiar person's voice, such as their key person or a parent. Gaze at faces, copying facial expressions and movements like sticking out their tongue. Make eye contact for longer periods. Watch someone's face as they talk. Copy what adults do, taking 'turns' in conversations (through babbling) and activities. Try to copy adult speech and lip movements. Enjoy singing, music and toys that make sounds. Recognise and are calmed by a familiar and friendly voice. Listen and respond to a simple instruction.	Babies and toddlers thrive when you show a genuine interest in them, join in and respond warmly. Using exaggerated intonation and a sing-song voice (infant-directed speech) helps babies tune in to language. Regularly using the babies and toddlers' names helps them to pay attention to what the practitioner is saying for example: "Chloe, have some milk." It is important to minimise background noise, so don't have music playing all the time. Babies love singing and music. Sing a range of songs and play a wide range of different types of music. Move with babies to music. Babies and toddlers love action rhymes and games like 'Peepo'. As they begin to join in with the words and the actions, they are developing their attention and listening. Allow babies time to anticipate words and actions in favourite songs.

Babies, toddlers and young children will be learning to:	Examples of how to support this:
  Observation checkpoint	**Around 6 months**, does the baby respond to familiar voices, turn to their own name and 'take turns' in conversations with babbling? **Around 12 months**, does the baby 'take turns' by babbling and using single words? Does the baby point to things and use gestures to show things to adults and share interests? **Around 18 months**, is the toddler listening and responding to a simple instruction like: "Adam, put on your shoes?"
Make sounds to get attention in different ways (for example, crying when hungry or unhappy, making gurgling sounds, laughing, cooing or babbling). Babble, using sounds like 'ba-ba', 'mamama'. Use gestures like waving and pointing to communicate.	Take time and 'tune in' to the messages babies are giving you through their vocalisations, body language and gestures. When babies and toddlers are holding and playing with objects, say what they are doing for example: "You've got the ball," and "Shake the rattle." 

Babies, toddlers and young children will be learning to:	Examples of how to support this:
Reach or point to something they want while making sounds. Copy your gestures and words. Constantly babble and use single words during play. Use intonation, pitch and changing volume when 'talking'.	Where you can, give meaning to the baby's gestures and pointing for example: "Oh, I see, you want the teddy." Chat with babies and toddlers all the time, but be careful not to overwhelm them with talk. Allow babies and toddlers to take the lead and then respond to their communications. Wait for the baby or toddler to speak or communicate with a sound or a look first — so that they are leading the conversation. When responding, expand on what has been said (for example, add a word). If a baby says "bottle", you could say "**milk** bottle". In a natural way, use the same word repeatedly in different contexts: "Look, a bottle of juice — oh, you've finished your bottle." Adding a word while a toddler is playing gives them the model of an expanded phrase. It also keeps the conversation on their topic of interest. Suggestion: if they say "bag", you could say: "Yes, daddy's bag".

Babies, toddlers and young children will be learning to:	Examples of how to support this:
 **Observation checkpoint**	Is the baby using speech sounds (babbling) to communicate with adults? **Around 12 months**: is the baby beginning to use single words like mummum, dada, tete (teddy)? **Around 15 months**, can the baby say around 10 words (they may not all be clear)? **Around 18 months**, is the toddler using a range of adult like speech patterns (jargon) and at least 20 clear words?
Understand single words in context — 'cup', 'milk', 'daddy'. Understand frequently used words such as 'all gone', 'no' and 'bye-bye'.	You can help babies with their understanding by using gestures and context. Suggestion: point to the cup and say "cup". Talking about what you are doing helps babies learn language in context. Suggestion: "I'm pouring out your milk into cup".
Observation checkpoint	Around 12 months, can the baby choose between 2 objects: "Do you want the ball or the car?"

Babies, toddlers and young children will be learning to:	Examples of how to support this:
Understand simple instructions like "give to mummy" or "stop". Recognise and point to objects if asked about them.	Singing, action rhymes and sharing books give children rich opportunities to understand new words. Play with groups of objects (different small world animals, or soft toys, or tea and picnic sets). Make sure you name things whilst playing, and talk about what you are doing
Observation checkpoint	Around 18 months, does the toddler understand lots of different single words and some two-word phrases, such as "give me" or "shoes on"?
Generally focus on an activity of their own choice and find it difficult to be directed by an adult.	Help toddlers and young children to focus their attention by using their name: "Fatima, put your coat on".
Listen to other people's talk with interest, but can easily be distracted by other things.	You can help toddlers and young children listen and pay attention by using gestures like pointing and facial expressions.

Babies, toddlers and young children will be learning to:	Examples of how to support this:
Can become frustrated when they can't make themselves understood. Start to say how they are feeling, using words as well as actions.	You can help toddlers who are having tantrums by being calm and reassuring. Help toddlers to express what's angering them by suggesting words to describe their emotions, like 'sad' or 'angry'. You can help further by explaining in simple terms why you think they may be feeling that emotion.
Start to develop conversation, often jumping from topic to topic. Develop pretend play: 'putting the baby to sleep' or 'driving the car to the shops'.	Make time to connect with babies, toddlers and young children. Tune in and listen to them and join in with their play, indoors and outside. Allow plenty of time to have conversations together, rather than busily rushing from one activity to the next. When you know a young child well, it is easier to understand them and talk about what their family life. For example: "OK, I see. You went to the shops with Aunty Maya".
Observation checkpoint	By around 2 years old, is the child showing an interest in what other children are playing and sometimes joins in? By around 3 years old, can the child shift from one task to another if you get their attention. Using the child's name can help: "Jason, can you stop now? We're tidying up".

Babies, toddlers and young children will be learning to:	Examples of how to support this:
Use the speech sounds p, b, m, w. Are usually still learning to pronounce: l/r/w/y f/th s/sh/ch/dz/j multi-syllabic words such as 'banana' and 'computer'	Toddlers and young children will pronounce some words incorrectly. Instead of correcting them, reply to what they say and use the words they have mispronounced. Children will then learn from your positive model, without losing the confidence to speak. Toddlers and young children sometimes hesitate and repeat sounds and words when thinking what to say. Listen patiently. Do not say the words for them. If the child or parents are distressed or worried by this, contact a speech and language therapist for advice. Encourage children to talk. Do not use too many questions: four comments to every question is a useful guide.
Observation checkpoint	**Towards their second birthday:** Can the child use up to 50 words? Is the child beginning to put two or three words together: "more milk"? Is the child frequently asking questions, such as the names of people and objects?

Babies, toddlers and young children will be learning to:	Examples of how to support this:
  Observation checkpoint	**Towards their third birthday:** Can the child use around 300 words? These words include descriptive language. They include words for time (for example, 'now' and 'later'), space (for example, 'over there') and function (for example, they can tell you a sponge is for washing). Is the child linking up to 5 words together? Is the child using pronouns ('me', 'him', 'she'), and using plurals and prepositions ('in', 'on', 'under') – these may not always be used correctly to start with. Can the child follow instructions with three key words like: "Can you wash dolly's face?"
Listen to simple stories and understand what is happening, with the help of the pictures.	Share picture books every day with children. Encourage them to talk about the pictures and the story. Comment on the pictures — for example: "It looks like the boy is a bit worried…" and wait for their response. You might also ask them about the pictures: "I wonder what the caterpillar is doing now?" Books with just pictures and no words can especially encourage conversations. Tell children the names of things they do not know and choose books that introduce interesting new vocabulary to them.

Babies, toddlers and young children will be learning to:	Examples of how to support this:
Identify familiar objects and properties for practitioners when they are described: for example: 'Katie's coat', 'blue car', 'shiny apple'. Understand and act on longer sentences like 'make teddy jump' or 'find your coat'.	When appropriate, you can check children's understanding by asking them to point to particular pictures. Or ask them to point to particular objects in a picture. For example: "Can you show me the big boat?"
Understand simple questions about 'who', 'what' and 'where' (but generally not 'why').	When talking with young children, give them plenty of processing time (at least 10 seconds). This gives them time to understand what you have said and think of their reply.
Observation checkpoint	**Around the age of 2**, can the child understand many more words than they can say – between 200–500 words? **Around the age of 2**, can the child understand simple questions and instructions like: "Where's your hat?" or "What's the boy in the picture doing?" **Around the age of 3**, can the child show that they understand action words by pointing to the right picture in a book. For example: "Who's jumping?" Note: watch out for children whose speech is not easily understood by unfamiliar adults. Monitor their progress and consider whether a hearing test might be needed.

3 & 4-year-olds will be learning to:	Examples of how to support this:
Enjoy listening to longer stories and can remember much of what happens. Can find it difficult to pay attention to more than one thing at a time.	Offer children at least a daily story time as well as sharing books throughout the session. If they are busy in their play, children may not be able to switch their attention and listen to what you say. When you need to, help young children to switch their attention from what they are doing to what you are saying. Give them a clear prompt. Suggestion: say the child's name and then: "Please stop and listen".
Use a wider range of vocabulary. Understand a question or instruction that has two parts, such as: "Get your coat and wait at the door". Understand 'why' questions, like: "Why do you think the caterpillar got so fat?"	Extend children's vocabulary, explaining unfamiliar words and concepts and making sure children have understood what they mean through stories and other activities. These should include words and concepts which occur frequently in books and other contexts, but are not used every day by many young children. Suggestion: use scientific vocabulary when talking about the parts of a flower or an insect, or different types of rocks. Examples from 'The Gruffalo' include: 'stroll', 'roasted', 'knobbly', 'wart' and 'feast'. Provide children with a rich language environment by sharing books and activities with them. Encourage children to talk about what is happening and give their own ideas. High-quality picture books are a rich source for learning new vocabulary and more complex forms of language: "Excuse me, I'm very hungry. Do you think I could have tea with you?"

3 & 4-year-olds will be learning to:	Examples of how to support this:
	Shared book-reading is a powerful way of having extended conversations with children. It helps children to build their vocabulary. Offer children lots of interesting things to investigate, like different living things. This will encourage them to ask questions.
Sing a large repertoire of songs. Know many rhymes, be able to talk about familiar books, and be able to tell a long story.	Consider which core books, songs and rhymes you want children to become familiar with and grow to love. Activities planned around those core books will help the children to practise the vocabulary and language from those books. It will also support their creativity and play. Suggestions: • Small world play based on 'Dear Zoo' will help children to learn the names of the different animals. Or they could shop for the different types of fruit in 'Handa's Surprise'. Pick them out and talk about how they look. This will help children to name the different types of fruit. Back in the setting, taste them and talk about their texture and smell. • Outdoor play themed around 'We're Going a Bear Hunt' might lead to the children creating their own 'hunts' and inventing their own rhymes.

3 & 4-year-olds will be learning to:	Examples of how to support this:
Develop their communication, but may continue to have problems with irregular tenses and plurals, such as 'runned' for 'ran', 'swimmed' for 'swam'. May have problems saying: some sounds: r, j, th, ch, and sh multisyllabic words such as 'pterodactyl', 'planetarium' or 'hippopotamus'.	Children may use ungrammatical forms like 'I swimmed'. Instead of correcting them, recast what the child said. For example: "How lovely that **you swam** in the sea on holiday". When children have difficulties with correct pronunciation, reply naturally to what they say. Pronounce the word correctly so they hear the correct model.
Use longer sentences of four to six words.	Expand on children's phrases. For example, if a child says, "going out shop", you could reply: "Yes, Jason is going to the shop". As well as adding language, add new ideas. For example: "I wonder if they'll get the 26 bus?" 

3 & 4-year-olds will be learning to:	Examples of how to support this:
Be able to express a point of view and to debate when they disagree with an adult or a friend, using words as well as actions. Can start a conversation with an adult or a friend and continue it for many turns. Use talk to organise themselves and their play: "Let's go on a bus... you sit there... I'll be the driver."	Model language that promotes thinking and challenges children: "I can see that's empty — I wonder what happened to the snail that used to be in that shell?" Open-ended questions like "I wonder what would happen if….?" encourage more thinking and longer responses. Sustained shared thinking is especially powerful. This is when two or more individuals (adult and child, or children) 'work together' in an intellectual way to solve a problem, clarify a concept, evaluate activities, extend a narrative etc. Help children to elaborate on how they are feeling: "You look sad. Are you upset because Jasmin doesn't want to do the same thing as you?" 

3 & 4-year-olds will be learning to:	Examples of how to support this:
Observation checkpoint	**Around the age of 3**, can the child shift from one task to another if you fully obtain their attention, for example, by using their name?
	Around the age of 4, is the child using sentences of four to six words — "I want to play with cars" or "What's that thing called?"?
	Can the child use sentences joined up with words like 'because', 'or', 'and'? For example: "I like ice cream because it makes my tongue shiver".
	Is the child using the future and past tense: "I am going to the park" and "I went to the shop"?
	Can the child answer simple 'why' questions?

Children in reception will be learning to:	Examples of how to support this:
Understand how to listen carefully and why listening is important.	Promote and model active listening skills: "Wait a minute, I need to get into a good position for listening, I can't see you. Let's be quiet so I can concentrate on what you're saying." Signal when you want children to listen: "Listen carefully now for how many animals are on the broom." Link listening with learning: "I could tell you were going to say the right answer, you were listening so carefully."
Learn new vocabulary.	Identify new vocabulary before planning activities, for example, changes in materials: 'dissolving', 'drying', 'evaporating'; in music: 'percussion', 'tambourine'. Bring in objects, pictures and photographs to talk about, for example vegetables to taste, smell and feel. Discuss which category the word is in, for example: "A cabbage is a kind of vegetable. It's a bit like a sprout but much bigger". Have fun saying the word in an exaggerated manner. Use picture cue cards to talk about an object: "What colour is it? Where would you find it? What shape is it? What does it smell like? What does it look like? What does it feel like? What does it sound like? What does it taste like?"

Children in reception will be learning to:	Examples of how to support this:
Use new vocabulary through the day.	Model words and phrases relevant to the area being taught, deliberately and systematically: "I'm thrilled that everyone's on time today", "I can see that you're delighted with your new trainers", "Stop shrieking, you're hurting my ears!", "What a downpour – I've never seen so much rain!", "It looks as if the sun has caused the puddles to evaporate", "Have you ever heard such a booming voice?" Use the vocabulary repeatedly through the week. Keep a list of previously taught vocabulary and review it in different contexts.
Ask questions to find out more and to check they understand what has been said to them.	Show genuine interest in knowing more: "This looks amazing, I need to know more about this." Think out loud, ask questions to check your understanding; make sure children can answer who, where and when questions before you move on to why and 'how do you know' questions: "I wonder why this jellyfish is so dangerous? Ahh, it has poison in its tentacles."

Children in reception will be learning to:	Examples of how to support this:
Articulate their ideas and thoughts in well-formed sentences.	Use complete sentences in your everyday talk. Help children build sentences using new vocabulary by rephrasing what they say and structuring their responses using sentence starters. Narrate your own and children's actions: "I've never seen so many beautiful bubbles, I can see all the colours of the rainbow in them." Build upon their incidental talk: "Your tower is definitely the tallest I've seen all week. Do you think you'll make it any higher?" Suggestion: ask open questions – "How did you make that? Why does the wheel move so easily? What will happen if you do that?" Instead of correcting, model accurate irregular grammar such as past tense, plurals, complex sentences: "That's right: you drank your milk quickly; you were quicker than Darren."

Children in reception will be learning to:	Examples of how to support this:
Connect one idea or action to another using a range of connectives.	Narrate events and actions: "I knew it must be cold outside because he was putting on his coat and hat."
	Remind children of previous events: "Do you remember when we forgot to wear our raincoats last week? It poured so much that we got drenched!"
	Extend their thinking: "You've thought really hard about building your tower, but how will you stop it falling down?"
Describe events in some detail.	Make deliberate mistakes highlighting to children that sometimes you might get it wrong: "It's important to get things in the right order so that people know what I'm talking about. Listen carefully to see if I have things in the right order: 'last week…'"
	Use sequencing words with emphasis in your own stories: "Before school I had a lovely big breakfast, then I had a chocolate biscuit at break time and after that I had two puddings for lunch. I'm so full!"

Children in reception will be learning to:	Examples of how to support this:
Use talk to help work out problems and organise thinking and activities explain how things work and why they might happen.	Think out loud how to work things out. Encourage children to talk about a problem together and come up with ideas for how to solve it. Give children problem solving words and phrases to use in their explanations: 'so that', 'because', 'I think it's...', 'you could...', 'it might be...'
Develop social phrases.	Model talk routines through the day. For example, arriving in school: "Good morning, how are you?"
Engage in storytimes.	Timetable a storytime at least once a day. Draw up a list of books that you enjoy reading aloud to children, including traditional and modern stories. Choose books that will develop their vocabulary. Display quality books in attractive book corners. Send home familiar and good-quality books for parents to read aloud and talk about with their children. Show parents how to share stories with their children.

Children in reception will be learning to:	Examples of how to support this:
Listen to and talk about stories to build familiarity and understanding.	Read and re-read selected stories. Show enjoyment of the story using your voice and manner to make the meaning clear. Use different voices for the narrator and each character. Make asides, commenting on what is happening in a story: "That looks dangerous — I'm sure they're all going to fall off that broom!" Link events in a story to your own experiences. Talk about the plot and the main problem in the story. Identify the main characters in the story, and talk about their feelings, actions and motives. Take on different roles in imaginative play, to interact and negotiate with people in longer conversations. Practise possible conversations between characters.
Retell the story, once they have developed a deep familiarity with the text; some as exact repetition and some in their own words.	Make familiar books available for children to share at school and at home. Make time for children to tell each other stories they have heard, or to visitors.

Children in reception will be learning to:	Examples of how to support this:
Use new vocabulary in different contexts.	Have fun with phrases from the story through the day: "I searched for a pencil, but no pencil could be found."
	Explain new vocabulary in the context of story, rather than in word lists.
Listen carefully to rhymes and songs, paying attention to how they sound.	Show your enjoyment of poems using your voice and manner to give emphasis to carefully chosen words and phrases.
	Model noticing how some words sound: "That poem was about a frog on a log; those words sound a bit the same at the end don't they? They rhyme."
	In poems and rhymes with very regular rhythm patterns, pause before the rhyming word to allow children to join in or predict the word coming next.
	Encourage children to have fun with rhyme, even if their suggestions don't make complete sense.
	Choose a few interesting longer words from the poem, rhyme or song and clap out their beat structure, helping children to join in with the correct number of 'claps'.

Children in reception will be learning to:	Examples of how to support this:
Learn rhymes, poems and songs.	Select traditional and contemporary poems and rhymes to read aloud to children. Help children to join in with refrains and learn some verses by heart using call and response. When singing songs by heart, talk about words in repeated phrases from within a refrain or verse so that word boundaries are noticed and not blurred: "Listen carefully, what words can you hear? Oncesuppona time: once – upon – a – time."
Engage in non-fiction books.	Read aloud books to children that will extend their knowledge of the world and illustrate a current topic. Select books containing photographs and pictures, for example, places in different weather conditions and seasons.
Listen to and talk about selected non-fiction to develop a deep familiarity with new knowledge and vocabulary.	Re-read some books so children learn the language necessary to talk about what is happening in each illustration and relate it to their own lives. Make the books available for children to share at school and at home.

Personal, Social and Emotional Development

Children's personal, social and emotional development (PSED) is crucial for children to lead healthy and happy lives, and is fundamental to their cognitive development. Underpinning their personal development are the important attachments that shape their social world. Strong, warm and supportive relationships with adults enable children to learn how to understand their own feelings and those of others. Children should be supported to manage emotions, develop a positive sense of self, set themselves simple goals, have confidence in their own abilities, to persist and wait for what they want and direct attention as necessary. Through adult modelling and guidance, they will learn how to look after their bodies, including healthy eating, and manage personal needs independently. Through supported interaction with other children they learn how to make good friendships, co-operate and resolve conflicts peaceably. These attributes will provide a secure platform from which children can achieve at school and in later life.

Statutory framework for the early years foundation stage: early adopter version

Babies, toddlers and young children will be learning to:	Examples of how to support this:
Find ways to calm themselves, through being calmed and comforted by their key person.	When settling a baby or toddler into nursery, the top priority is for the key person to develop a strong and loving relationship with the young child. Learn from the family about what they do to soothe their child and what to look out for — for example, a baby who scratches at their head when they are getting tired. Find out what calms a baby — rocking, cuddling or singing. Make sure babies and toddlers can get hold of their comfort object when they need it. Explain to parents that once babies establish 'object permanence', they become more aware of the presence or absence of their parents. Object permanence means knowing that something continues to exist even when out of sight. This can make separations much more distressing and difficult between 6–24 months.
Establish their sense of self.	Babies develop a sense of self by interacting with others, and by exploring their bodies and objects around them, inside and outdoors. Respond and build on babies' expressions and gestures, playfully exploring the idea of self/other. Suggestion: point to your own nose/eyes/mouth, point to the baby's.

Babies, toddlers and young children will be learning to:	Examples of how to support this:
Express preferences and decisions. They also try new things and start establishing their autonomy. Engage with others through gestures, gaze and talk. Use that engagement to achieve a goal. For example, gesture towards their cup to say they want a drink.	Be positive and interested in what babies do as they develop their confidence in trying new things. Help toddlers and young children to make informed choices from a limited range of options. Suggestion: enable children to choose which song to sing from a set of four song cards, by pointing. Enable children to choose whether they want milk or water at snack time.
Find ways of managing transitions, for example from their parent to their key person.	Support children as they find their own different ways to manage feelings of sadness when their parents leave them. Some children might need to hold onto a special object from home to feel strong and confident in the setting. Some might need to snuggle in and be comforted by their key person. Some might get busy straight away in their favourite play or with another child they feel close to. Young children need to feel secure as they manage difficult emotions. Provide consistent and predicable routines, with flexibility when needed.

Babies, toddlers and young children will be learning to:	Examples of how to support this:
Thrive as they develop self-assurance.	Provide consistent, warm and responsive care. At first, centre this on the key person. In time, children can develop positive relationships with other adults. When the key person is not available, make sure that someone familiar provides comfort and support, and carries out intimate care routines.
Look back as they crawl or walk away from their key person. Look for clues about how to respond to something interesting. Play with increasing confidence on their own and with other children, because they know their key person is nearby and available. Feel confident when taken out around the local neighbourhood, and enjoy exploring new places with their key person.	Acknowledge babies' and toddlers' brief need for reassurance as they move away from their key person. Encourage babies and toddlers to explore, indoors and outside. Help them to become more independent by smiling and looking encouraging, for example when a baby keeps crawling towards a rattle. Arrange resources inside and outdoors to encourage children's independence and growing self-confidence. Suggestion: Treasure Basket play allows babies who can sit up to choose what to play with. Store resources so that children can access them freely, without needing help.
Feel strong enough to express a range of emotions.	Help children to feel emotionally safe with a key person and, gradually, with other members of staff.

Babies, toddlers and young children will be learning to:	Examples of how to support this:
Grow in independence, rejecting help ("me do it "). Sometimes this leads to feelings of frustration and tantrums.	Show warmth and affection, combined with clear and appropriate boundaries and routines. Develop a spirit of friendly co-operation amongst children and adults. Encourage children to express their feelings through words like 'sad', 'upset' or 'angry'. Toddlers and young children may have periods of time when their favourite word is 'no' and when they want to carry out their wishes straight away. Maintain sensible routines and boundaries for children during these testing times. Negative or harsh responses can cause children to feel unduly anxious and emotionally vulnerable. Offer supervision or work discussion sessions to staff. Staff will need to talk about the strong feelings that children may express. How are practitioners feeling about these and developing their understanding of the children's feelings? 

Babies, toddlers and young children will be learning to:	Examples of how to support this:
Begin to show 'effortful control'. For example, waiting for a turn and resisting the strong impulse to grab what they want or push their way to the front. Be increasingly able to talk about and manage their emotions.	When appropriate, notice and talk about children's feelings. For example: "I can see it's hard to wait, just a minute and then it's your turn to go down the slide." Model useful phrases like "Can I have a turn?" or "My turn next."
Notice and ask questions about differences, such as skin colour, types of hair, gender, special needs and disabilities, and so on.	Be open to what children say about differences and answer their questions straightforwardly. Help children develop positive attitudes towards diversity and inclusion. Help all children to feel that they are valued, and they belong.
Develop friendships with other children.	Support children to find ways into the play and friendship groups of others. For example, encourage them to stand and watch from the side with you. Talk about what you see, and suggest ways for the child to join in.
Safely explore emotions beyond their normal range through play and stories.	Story times with props can engage children in a range of emotions. They can feel the family's fear as the bear chases them at the end of 'We're Going on a Bear Hunt'. They can feel relief when the Gruffalo is scared away by the mouse.

Babies, toddlers and young children will be learning to:	Examples of how to support this:
Are talking about their feelings in more elaborated ways: "I'm sad because…" or "I love it when …".	Recognise, talk about and expand on children's emotions. For example, you might say: "Sara is smiling. She really wanted a turn with the truck."
![magnifying glass] **Observation checkpoint**	**Around 7 months**, does the baby respond to their name and respond to the emotions in your voice? **Around 12 months**, does the baby start to be shy around strangers and show preferences for certain people and toys? **Around 18 months**, is the toddler increasingly curious about their world and wanting to explore it and be noticed by you? **Around the age of 2**, does the child start to see themselves as a separate person? For example, do they decide what to play with, what to eat, what to wear? **Between the ages of 2 and 3**, does the child start to enjoy the company of other children and want to play with them? **Note**: watch out for children who get extremely upset by certain sounds, smells or tastes, and cannot be calmed. Or children who seem worried, sad or angry for much of the time. You will need to work closely with parents and other agencies to find out more about these developmental difficulties.

3 & 4-year-olds will be learning to:	Examples of how to support this:
Select and use activities and resources, with help when needed. This helps them to achieve a goal they have chosen, or one which is suggested to them.	Respond to children's increasing independence and sense of responsibility. As the year proceeds, increase the range of resources and challenges, outdoors and inside. One example of this might be starting the year with light hammers, plastic golf tees and playdough. This equipment will offer children a safe experience of hammering. Wait until the children are ready to follow instructions and use tools safely. Then you could introduce hammers with short handles, nails with large heads, and soft blocks of wood. Widen the range of activities that children feel confident to take part in, outdoors and inside. Model inviting new activities that encourage children to come over and join in, such as folding paper to make animals, sewing or weaving.
Develop their sense of responsibility and membership of a community.	Give children appropriate tasks to carry out. Suggestion: they can fetch milk cartons or fruit. They can wash up their own plates after their snack.
Become more outgoing with unfamiliar people, in the safe context of their setting. Show more confidence in new social situations.	Invite trusted people into the setting to talk about and show the work they do. Some examples of this might be plumbers, artists or firefighters. Take children out on short walks around the neighbourhood. When ready, take them on trips to interesting places like a local museum, theatre or place of worship.

3 & 4-year-olds will be learning to:	Examples of how to support this:
Play with one or more other children, extending and elaborating play ideas. Help to find solutions to conflicts and rivalries. For example, accepting that not everyone can be Spider-Man in the game, and suggesting other ideas.	Involve children in making decisions about room layout and resources. Suggestion: you could set up a special role-play area in response to children's fascination with space. Support children to carry out decisions, respecting the wishes of the rest of the group. Further resource and enrich children's play, based on their interests. Suggestion: children often like to talk about their trips to hairdressers and barbers. You could provide wigs reflecting different ethnicities, combs and brushes etc. to stimulate pretend play around their interest. Notice children who find it difficult to play. They may need extra help to share and manage conflicts. You could set up play opportunities in quiet spaces for them, with just one or two other children. You may need to model positive play and co-operation. Teach children ways of solving conflicts. Suggestion: model how to listen to someone else and agree a compromise.
Increasingly follow rules, understanding why they are important. Do not always need an adult to remind them of a rule.	Explain why we have rules and display a small number of necessary rules visually as reminders. Suggestion: display a photo showing a child taking just one piece of fruit at the snack table.

3 & 4-year-olds will be learning to:	Examples of how to support this:
Develop appropriate ways of being assertive. Talk with others to solve conflicts. Talk about their feelings using words like 'happy', 'sad', 'angry' or 'worried'.	Children with high levels of negative emotion need clear boundaries and routines. They also need practitioners to interact calmly and sensitively with them. Model ways that you calm yourself down, such as stopping and taking a few deep breaths. This can help children to learning ways to calm themselves. If adults are excessively challenging or controlling, children can become more aggressive in the group. They may increasingly 'act out' their feelings. For example, when they feel sad, they might hit another child to make that child feel sad as well.
Begin to understand how others might be feeling.	Help children explore situations from different points of view. Talk together about how others might be feeling. Bring these ideas into children's pretend play: "I wonder how the chicken is feeling, now the fox is creeping up on her?"

3 & 4-year-olds will be learning to:	Examples of how to support this:
Observation checkpoint	**Around the age of 3** Can the child sometimes manage to share or take turns with others, with adult guidance and understanding 'yours' and 'mine'? Can the child settle to some activities for a while? **Around the age of 4** Does the child play alongside others or do they always want to play alone? Does the child take part in pretend play (for example, being 'mummy' or 'daddy'?) Does the child take part in other pretend play with different roles — being the Gruffalo, for example? Can the child generally negotiate solutions to conflicts in their play? **Note**: watch out for children who seem worried, sad or angry for much of the time, children who seem to flit from one thing to the next or children who seem to stay for over-long periods doing the same thing, and become distressed if they are encouraged to do something different You will need to work closely with parents and other agencies to find out more about these developmental difficulties.

Children in reception will be learning to:	Examples of how to support this:
See themselves as a valuable individual.	Make time to get to know the child and their family. Ask parents about the child's history, likes, dislikes, family members and culture. Take opportunities in class to highlight a child's interests, showing you know them and about them.
Build constructive and respectful relationships.	Make sure children are encouraged to listen to each other as well as the staff. Ensure children's play regularly involves sharing and cooperating with friends and other peers. Congratulate children for their kindness to others and express your approval when they help, listen and support each other. Allow children time in friendship groups as well as other groupings. Have high expectations for children following instructions, with high levels of support when necessary.

Children in reception will be learning to:	Examples of how to support this:
Express their feelings and consider the feelings of others.	Model positive behaviour and highlight exemplary behaviour of children in class, narrating what was kind and considerate about the behaviour.

Encourage children to express their feelings if they feel hurt or upset using descriptive vocabulary. Help and reassure them when they are distressed, upset or confused.

Undertake specific activities that encourage about talk about feelings and their opinions. |
| Show resilience and perseverance in the face of challenge. | Offer constructive support and recognition of child's personal achievements.

Provide opportunities for children to tell each other about their work and play. Help them reflect and self-evaluate their own work.

Help them to develop problem-solving skills by talking through how they, you and others resolved a problem or difficulty. Show that mistakes are an important part of learning and going back is trial and error not failure.

Help children to set own goals and to achieve them. |

Children in reception will be learning to:	Examples of how to support this:
Identify and moderate their own feelings socially and emotionally.	Give children strategies for staying calm in the face of frustration. Talk them through why we take turns, wait politely, tidy up after ourselves and so on. Encourage them to think about their own feelings those of others by giving explicit examples of how others might feel in particular scenarios. Give children space to calm down and return to an activity. Support all children to recognise when their behaviour was not in accordance with the rules and why it is important to respect class rules and behave correctly towards others.
Think about the perspectives of others.	Use dialogic story time (talking about the ideas arising from the story whilst reading aloud) to discuss books that deal with challenges, explaining how the different characters feel about these challenges and overcome them. Ask children to explain to others how they thought about a problem or an emotion and how they dealt with it.
Manage their own needs.	Model practices that support good hygiene, such as insisting on washing hands before snack time. Narrating your own decisions about healthy foods, highlighting the importance of eating plenty of fruits and vegetables.

Physical Development

Physical activity is vital in children's all-round development, enabling them to pursue happy, healthy and active lives. Gross and fine motor experiences develop incrementally throughout early childhood, starting with sensory explorations and the development of a child's strength, co-ordination and positional awareness through tummy time, crawling and play movement with both objects and adults. By creating games and providing opportunities for play both indoors and outdoors, adults can support children to develop their core strength, stability, balance, spatial awareness, co-ordination and agility. Gross motor skills provide the foundation for developing healthy bodies and social and emotional well-being. Fine motor control and precision helps with hand-eye co-ordination which is later linked to early literacy. Repeated and varied opportunities to explore and play with small world activities, puzzles, arts and crafts and the practise of using small tools, with feedback and support from adults, allow children to develop proficiency, control and confidence.

Statutory framework for the early years foundation stage: early adopter version

Birth to three – babies, toddlers and young children will be learning to:	Examples of how to support this:
Lift their head while lying on their front. Push their chest up with straight arms. Roll over: from front to back, then back to front. Enjoy moving when outdoors and inside.	Some babies need constant physical contact, attention and physical intimacy. Respond warmly and patiently to them. Provide adequate, clean floor space for babies to experience tummy-time and back time. Offer this frequently throughout the day so that they can develop their gross motor skills (kicking, waving, rolling and reaching).
Sit without support. Begin to crawl in different ways and directions. Pull themselves upright and bouncing in preparation for walking.	Encourage babies to sit on you, climb over you, and rock, bounce or sway with you. Notice, cherish and applaud the physical achievements of babies and toddlers. Give babies time to move freely during care routines, like nappy-changing. Encourage independence. Suggestion: offer a range of opportunities for children to move by themselves, making their own decisions about direction and speed.

Birth to three – babies, toddlers and young children will be learning to:	Examples of how to support this:
Reach out for objects as co-ordination develops. Eat finger food and develop likes and dislikes. Try a wider range of foods with different tastes and textures. Lift objects up to suck them. Pass things from one hand to the other. Let go of things and hands them to another person, or drops them.	Gradually share control of the bottle with young babies. Introduce children regularly and repeatedly to new foods, being positive and patient as they try new things. Value the choices children make, whilst also sensitively encouraging them to try healthy foods. Consider introducing a supervised toothbrushing programme. Use everyday, open-ended materials to support overall co-ordination. Suggestions: sponges and cloths to hold, squash and throw, or wet and squeeze. Provide a range of surfaces and materials for babies to explore, stimulating touch and all the senses. 

Birth to three – babies, toddlers and young children will be learning to:	Examples of how to support this:
  Observation checkpoint	Does the baby move with ease and enjoyment? **At around 12 months:** Can the baby pull to stand from a sitting position and sit down? Can the baby pick up something small with their first finger and thumb (such as a piece of string)? **Note:** look out for babies and young toddlers who appear underweight, overweight or to have poor dental health. You will need to work closely with parents and health visitors to help improve the child's health.
Gradually gain control of their whole body through continual practice of large movements, such as waving, kicking, rolling, crawling and walking. Clap and stamp to music. Fit themselves into spaces, like tunnels, dens and large boxes, and move around in them. Enjoy starting to kick, throw and catch balls.	Provide a wide range of opportunities for children to move throughout the day: indoors and outside, alone or with others, with and without apparatus. Include risky and rough and tumble play, as appropriate. Join in with children's movement play when invited and if it is appropriate. Then you can show different ways of moving and engaging with the resources. Help young children learn what physical risks they are confident and able to take. Encourage children to climb unaided and to stop if they do not feel safe. If you lift them onto the apparatus and hold them so they balance, they will not develop a sense of what they can do safely.

Birth to three – babies, toddlers and young children will be learning to:	Examples of how to support this:
Build independently with a range of appropriate resources.	Offer outdoor play every day for at least 45 minutes. Include lots of opportunities for children to move freely and explore their surroundings like a slope, a large hole, puddles or a sandpit. Consider wider opportunities for movement. Suggestions: using large moveable resources like hollow blocks, swinging on monkey bars, soft play, climbing walls, crawling into tunnels and dens. Consider going to suitable local facilities.
Begin to walk independently – choosing appropriate props to support at first. Walk, run, jump and climb – and start to use the stairs independently.	As soon as children are able, encourage 'active travel' to and from the setting – for example, walking, scooter or bike.
Spin, roll and independently use ropes and swings (for example, tyre swings). Sit on a push-along wheeled toy, use a scooter or ride a tricycle.	Provide materials and equipment that support physical development – both large and small motor skills. Encourage children to use materials flexibly and combine them in different ways. Check that children's clothing and footwear are not too tight or too large.

Birth to three – babies, toddlers and young children will be learning to:	Examples of how to support this:
Observation checkpoint	**Around their second birthday**, can the toddler run well, kick a ball, and jump with both feet off the ground at the same time? **Around their third birthday**, can the child climb confidently, catch a large ball and pedal a tricycle?
Develop manipulation and control. Explore different materials and tools.	Provide different types of paper for children to tear, make marks on and print on. Provide lots of different things for young children to grasp, hold and explore, like clay, finger paint, spoons, brushes, shells.
Use large and small motor skills to do things independently, for example manage buttons and zips, and pour drinks. Show an increasing desire to be independent, such as wanting to feed themselves and dress or undress.	Provide babies and toddlers with lots of opportunities to feed themselves. Encourage them to dress and undress independently. Be patient, do not rush and take time to talk about what they are doing and why: "It's a bit cold and wet today — what do we need to wear to keep warm and dry?" At meal and snack times, encourage children to try a range of foods as they become more independent eaters. Encourage children to help with carrying, pouring drinks, cleaning and sorting. Encourage young children's personal decision-making by offering real choices — water or milk, for example. They can comment on how to eat healthily, listen to children's responses and develop conversations about this.

Birth to three – babies, toddlers and young children will be learning to:	Examples of how to support this:
Use large and small motor skills to do things independently, for example manage buttons and zips, and pour drinks. Show an increasing desire to be independent, such as wanting to feed themselves and dress or undress.	Encourage good eating habits and behaviours, such as not snatching, sharing and waiting for a second helping.
  Observation checkpoint	Look out for children who find it difficult to sit comfortably on chairs. They may need help to develop their core muscles. You can help them by encouraging them to scoot on sit-down trikes without pedals, and jump on soft-play equipment. 

Birth to three – babies, toddlers and young children will be learning to:	Examples of how to support this:
Learn to use the toilet with help, and then independently.	You cannot force a child to use the potty or toilet. You need to establish friendly co-operation with the child. That will help them take this important step. Children can generally control their bowels before their bladder. Notice when young children are ready to begin toilet training and discuss this with their parents: • they know when they have got a wet or dirty nappy • they get to know when they are peeing and may tell you they are doing it • the gap between wetting is at least an hour • they show they need to pee by fidgeting or going somewhere quiet or hidden • they know when they need to pee and may say so in advance Potty training is fastest if you start it when the child is at the last stage. By the age of 3, 9 out of 10 children are dry most days. All children will have the occasional 'accident', though, especially when excited, busy or upset.

3 & 4-year-olds will be learning to:	Examples of how to support this:
Continue to develop their movement, balancing, riding (scooters, trikes and bikes) and ball skills. Go up steps and stairs, or climb up apparatus, using alternate feet. Skip, hop, stand on one leg and hold a pose for a game like musical statues. Use large-muscle movements to wave flags and streamers, paint and make marks.	Encourage children to transfer physical skills learnt in one context to another one. Suggestion: children might first learn to hammer in pegs to mark their Forest school boundary, using a mallet. Then, they are ready to learn how to use hammers and nails at the woodwork bench. Encourage children to paint, chalk or make marks with water on large vertical surfaces. Suggestion: use walls as well as easels to stimulate large shoulder and arm movements. These experiences help children to 'cross the mid-line' of their bodies. When they draw a single line from left to right, say, they don't need to pass the paintbrush from one hand to another or have to move their whole body along.
Start taking part in some group activities which they make up for themselves, or in teams. Are increasingly able to use and remember sequences and patterns of movements which are related to music and rhythm.	Lead movement-play activities when appropriate. These will challenge and enhance children's physical skills and development — using both fixed and flexible resources, indoors and outside. Model the vocabulary of movement — 'gallop', 'slither' — and encourage children to use it. Also model the vocabulary of instruction — 'follow', 'lead', 'copy' — and encourage children to use it.
Match their developing physical skills to tasks and activities in the setting. For example, they decide whether to crawl, walk or run across a plank, depending on its length and width.	Encourage children to become more confident, competent, creative and adaptive movers. Then, extend their learning by providing opportunities to play outdoors in larger areas, such as larger parks and spaces in the local area, or through Forest or Beach school.

3 & 4-year-olds will be learning to:	Examples of how to support this:
Choose the right resources to carry out their own plan. For example, choosing a spade to enlarge a small hole they dug with a trowel. Collaborate with others to manage large items, such as moving a long plank safely, carrying large hollow blocks.	Explain why safety is an important factor in handling tools, and moving equipment and materials. Have clear and sensible rules for everybody to follow.
  Observation checkpoint	Look out for children who appear to be overweight or to have poor dental health, where this has not been picked up and acted on at an earlier health check. Discuss this sensitively with parents and involve the child's health visitor. Adapt activities to suit their particular needs, so all children feel confident to move and take part in physical play.
Use one-handed tools and equipment, for example, making snips in paper with scissors. Use a comfortable grip with good control when holding pens and pencils. Start to eat independently and learning how to use a knife and fork. Show a preference for a dominant hand.	You can begin by showing children how to use one-handed tools (scissors and hammers, for example) and then guide them with hand-over-hand help. Gradually reduce the help you are giving and allow the child to use the tool independently. The tripod grip is a comfortable way to hold a pencil or pen. It gives the child good control. The pen is pinched between the ball of the thumb and the fore-finger, supported by the middle finger with the other fingers tucked into the hand. You can help children to develop this grip with specially designed pens and pencils, or grippers. Encourage children to pick up small objects like individual gravel stones or tiny bits of chalk to draw with.

3 & 4-year-olds will be learning to:	Examples of how to support this:
Be increasingly independent as they get dressed and undressed, for example, putting coats on and doing up zips. Be increasingly independent in meeting their own care needs, e.g. brushing teeth, using the toilet, washing and drying their hands thoroughly. Make healthy choices about food, drink, activity and toothbrushing.	Encourage children by helping them, but leaving them to do the last steps, such as pulling up their zip after you have started it off. Gradually reduce your help until the child can do each step on their own. Talk to children about the importance of eating healthily and brushing their teeth. Consider how to support oral health. For example, some settings use a toothbrushing programme. Talk to children about why it's important to wash their hands carefully and throughout the day, including before they eat and after they've used the toilet.
Observation checkpoint	Most, but not all, children are reliably dry during the day by the age of 4. Support children who are struggling with toilet training, in partnership with their parents. Seek medical advice, if necessary, from a health visitor or GP.

Children in reception will be learning to:	Examples of how to support this:

Revise and refine the fundamental movement skills they have already acquired:
 	
   • rolling
 	
   • crawling
 	
   • walking
 	
   • jumping
 	
   • running
 	
   • hopping
 	
   • skipping
 	
   • climbing
	Provide regular access to appropriate outdoor space. Ensure there is a range of surfaces to feel, move and balance on, such as grass, earth and bark chippings.
	
	Give children experience of carrying things up and down on different levels (slopes, hills and steps).
	
	Provide a choice of open-ended materials to play that allow for extended, repeated and regular practising of physical skills like lifting, carrying, pushing, pulling, constructing, stacking and climbing.
	
	Provide regular access to floor space indoors for movement.
	
	Ensure that spaces are accessible to children with varying confidence levels, skills and needs.
	
	Provide a wide range of activities to support a broad range of abilities.
	
	Allow less competent and confident children to spend time initially observing and listening, without feeling pressured to join in.
	
	Create low-pressure zones where less confident children can practise movement skills on their own, or with one or two others.
	
	Model precise vocabulary to describe movement and directionality, and encourage children to use it.

Children in reception will be learning to:	Examples of how to support this:
Progress towards a more fluent style of moving, with developing control and grace.	Provide children with regular opportunities to practise their movement skills alone and with others. Offer children further physical challenges when they are ready, such as climbing higher, running faster and jumping further. Encourage children to conclude movements in balance and stillness. Allow for time to be still and quiet. Suggestion: looking up at the sky, or sitting or lying in a den.
Develop the overall body strength, co-ordination, balance and agility needed to engage successfully with future physical education sessions and other physical disciplines including dance, gymnastics, sport and swimming.	Encourage children to be highly active and get out of breath several times every day. Provide opportunities for children to, spin, rock, tilt, fall, slide and bounce. Provide a range of wheeled resources for children to balance, sit or ride on, or pull and push. Two-wheeled balance bikes and pedal bikes without stabilisers, skateboards, wheelbarrows, prams and carts are all good options.
Develop their small motor skills so that they can use a range of tools	Before teaching children the correct pencil grip and posture for writing, or how to use a knife and fork and cut with scissors, check:

Children in reception will be learning to:	Examples of how to support this:
competently, safely and confidently. Suggested tools: pencils for drawing and writing, paintbrushes, scissors, knives, forks and spoons.	<ul><li>that children have developed their upper arm and shoulder strength sufficiently: they don't need to move their shoulders as they move their hands and fingers</li><li>that they can move and rotate their lower arms and wrists independently</li></ul>Help children to develop the core strength and stability they need to support their small motor skills. Encourage and model tummy-crawling, crawling on all fours, climbing, pulling themselves up on a rope and hanging on monkey bars. Offer children activities to develop and further refine their small motor skills. Suggestions: threading and sewing, woodwork, pouring, stirring, dancing with scarves, using spray bottles, dressing and undressing dolls, planting and caring for plants, playing with small world toys, and making models with junk materials, construction kits and malleable materials like clay. Regularly review the equipment for children to develop their small motor skills. Is it appropriate for the different levels of skill and confidence of children in the class? Is it challenging for the most dexterous children? Continuously check how children are holding pencils for writing, scissors and knives and forks. Offer regular, gentle encouragement and feedback. With regular practice, the physical skills children need to eat with a knife and fork and develop an efficient handwriting style will become increasingly automatic.

Children in reception will be learning to:	Examples of how to support this:
Develop their small motor skills so that they can use a range of tools competently, safely and confidently. Suggested tools: pencils for drawing and writing, paintbrushes, scissors, knives, forks and spoons. (continued)	
Use their core muscle strength to achieve a good posture when sitting at a table or sitting on the floor.	Provide areas for sitting at a table that are quiet, purposeful and free of distraction. Give children regular, sensitive reminders about correct posture. Provide different chairs at the correct height for the range of children in the class, so that their feet are flat on the floor or a footrest. Provide different tables at the correct height for the range of children in the class. The table supports children's forearms. The top of the table is slightly higher than the height of the child's elbow flexed to 90 degrees.

Children in reception will be learning to:	Examples of how to support this:
Combine different movements with ease and fluency.	Create obstacle courses that demand a range of movements to complete, such as crawling through a tunnel, climbing onto a chair, jumping into a hoop and running and lying on a cushion. Provide opportunities to move that require quick changes of speed and direction. Suggestions: run around in a circle, stop, change direction and walk on your knees going the other way. Encourage precision and accuracy when beginning and ending movements.
Confidently and safely use a range of large and small apparatus indoors and outside, alone and in a group. Develop overall body-strength, balance, co-ordination and agility.	Encourage children to use a range of equipment. These might include: wheeled toys, wheelbarrows, tumbling mats, ropes to pull up on, spinning cones, tunnels, tyres, structures to jump on/off, den-making materials, logs and planks to balance on, A-frames and ladders, climbing walls, slides and monkey bars. 

Children in reception will be learning to:	Examples of how to support this:
Further develop and refine a range of ball skills including: throwing, catching, kicking, passing, batting, and aiming. Develop confidence, competence, precision and accuracy when engaging in activities that involve a ball.	Provide a range of different sized 'balls' made out of familiar materials like socks, paper bags and jumpers that are softer and slower than real balls. Introduce full-sized balls when children are confident to engage with them. Introduce tennis balls, ping pong balls, beach balls and balloons. Introduce a range of resources used to bat, pat and hit a ball, modelling how to do this and giving children plenty of time for practice. Introduce children to balls games with teams, rules and targets when they have consolidated their ball skills.
Develop the foundations of a handwriting style which is fast, accurate and efficient.	Encourage children to draw freely. Engage children in structured activities: guide them in what to draw, write or copy. Teach and model correct letter formation. Continuously check the process of children's handwriting (pencil grip and letter formation, including directionality). Provide extra help and guidance when needed. Plan for regular repetition so that correct letter formation becomes automatic, efficient and fluent over time.

Children in reception will be learning to:	Examples of how to support this:
Know and talk about the different factors that support their overall health and wellbeing: • regular physical activity • healthy eating • toothbrushing • sensible amounts of 'screen time' • having a good sleep routine • being a safe pedestrian	Talk with children about exercise, healthy eating and the importance of sleep. Use picture books and other resources to explain the importance of the different aspects of a healthy lifestyle. Explain to children and model how to travel safely in their local environment, including: staying on the pavement, holding hands and crossing the road when walking, stopping quickly when scootering and cycling, and being sensitive to other pedestrians. 

Children in reception will be learning to:	Examples of how to support this:
Further develop the skills they need to manage the school day successfully: • lining up and queuing • mealtimes • personal hygiene	Carefully explain some of the rules of lining up and queuing, such as not standing too close or touching others. Give children simple verbal and visual reminders. Celebrate, praise and reward children as they develop patience, turn-taking and self-control when they need to line up and wait. Teach and model for children how to eat with good manners in a group, taking turns and being considerate to others. Help individual children to develop good personal hygiene. Acknowledge and praise their efforts. Provide regular reminders about thorough handwashing and toileting. Work with parents and health visitors or the school nurse to help children who are not usually clean and dry through the day.

Literacy

It is crucial for children to develop a life-long love of reading. Reading consists of two dimensions: language comprehension and word reading. Language comprehension (necessary for both reading and writing) starts from birth. It only develops when adults talk with children about the world around them and the books (stories and non-fiction) they read with them, and enjoy rhymes, poems and songs together. Skilled word reading, taught later, involves both the speedy working out of the pronunciation of unfamiliar printed words (decoding) and the speedy recognition of familiar printed words. Writing involves transcription (spelling and handwriting) and composition (articulating ideas and structuring them in speech, before writing).

Statutory framework for the early years foundation stage: early adopter version

Babies, toddlers and young children will be learning to:	Examples of how to support this:
Enjoy songs and rhymes, tuning in and paying attention. Join in with songs and rhymes, copying sounds, rhythms, tunes and tempo. Say some of the words in songs and rhymes. Copy finger movements and other gestures. Sing songs and say rhymes independently, for example, singing whilst playing.	Song and rhyme times can happen spontaneously throughout the day, indoors and outside, with individual children, in pairs or in small groups. You can make song and rhyme times engaging for young children by using a wide range of props or simple instruments. Children can choose the songs and rhymes they would like to join in with, using picture cards or by speaking You could learn songs and rhymes from parents. You could also teach parents the songs and rhymes you use in the setting, in order to support learning at home. Choose songs and rhymes which reflect the range of cultures and languages of children in the twenty-first century. 

143

Babies, toddlers and young children will be learning to:	Examples of how to support this:
Enjoy sharing books with an adult. Pay attention and responds to the pictures or the words. Have favourite books and seek them out, to share with an adult, with another child, or to look at alone. Repeat words and phrases from familiar stories. Ask questions about the book. Makes comments and shares their own ideas. Develop play around favourite stories using props.	Provide enticing areas for sharing books, stocked with a wide range of high-quality books, matching the many different interests of children in the setting. Provide a comfortable place for sharing books, like a sofa. In warm weather, share books outside on a picnic rug or in small tents. Themed book areas can build on children's interests. Suggestions: relevant books close to small world play about dinosaurs, or cookbooks in the home corner. Help children to explore favourite books through linked activities. Suggestions: • visiting the park or the countryside to splash through puddles and squelch through mud for 'We're Going on a Bear Hunt' • going out to buy chillies for 'Lima's Red Hot Chilli' • dressing up clothes and small world play for favourite books
Notice some print, such as the first letter of their name, a bus or door number, or a familiar logo.	Point out print in the environment and talk about what it means. Suggestions: on a local walk, point out road signs, shop names and door numbers.

Babies, toddlers and young children will be learning to:	Examples of how to support this:
Enjoy drawing freely. Add some marks to their drawings, which they give meaning to. For example: "That says mummy." Make marks on their picture to stand for their name.	Provide a wide range of stimulating equipment to encourage children's mark-making. Suggestions: • large-scale sensory play, such as making marks with fingers in wet sand or in a tray of flour • using sticks and leaves to make marks during Forest school sessions • large brushes with paint or water • dragging streamers through puddles. Once large-muscle co-ordination is developing well, children can develop small-muscle co-ordination Playground chalk, smaller brushes, pencils and felt pens will support this.

3 & 4-year-olds will be learning to:	Examples of how to support this:
Understand the five key concepts about print: • print has meaning • print can have different purposes • we read English text from left to right and from top to bottom • the names of the different parts of a book • page sequencing	Draw children's attention to a wide range of examples of print with different functions. These could be a sign to indicate a bus stop or to show danger, a menu for choosing what you want to eat, or a logo that stands for a particular shop. When reading to children, sensitively draw their attention to the parts of the books, for example, the cover, the author, the page number. Show children how to handle books and to turn the pages one at a time. Show children where the text is, and how English print is read left to right and top to bottom. Show children how sentences start with capital letters and end with full stops. Explain the idea of a 'word' to children, pointing out how some words are longer than others and how there is always a space before and after a word. 

3 & 4-year-olds will be learning to:	Examples of how to support this:
Develop their phonological awareness, so that they can: • spot and suggest rhymes • count or clap syllables in a word • recognise words with the same initial sound, such as money and mother	Help children tune into the different sounds in English by making changes to rhymes and songs, like: • changing a word so that there is still a rhyme: "Twinkle, twinkle chocolate bar" • making rhymes personal to children: "Hey diddle diddle, the cat and fiddle, the cow jumped over Haroon." Deliberately miss out a word in a rhyme, so the children have to fill it in: "Run, run, as fast as you can, you can't catch me I'm the gingerbread —." Use magnet letters to spell a word ending like 'at'. Encourage children to put other letters in front to create rhyming words like 'hat' and 'cat'.
Engage in extended conversations about stories, learning new vocabulary.	Choose books which reflect diversity. Regular sharing of books and discussion of children's ideas and responses (dialogic reading) helps children to develop their early enjoyment and understanding of books. Simple picture books, including those with no text, can be powerful ways of learning new vocabulary (for example, naming what's in the picture). More complex stories will help children to learn a wider range of vocabulary. This type of vocabulary is not in everyday use, but occurs frequently in books and other contexts. Examples include: 'caterpillar', 'enormous', 'forest', 'roar' and 'invitation'.

3 & 4-year-olds will be learning to:	Examples of how to support this:
Use some of their print and letter knowledge in their early writing. For example: writing a pretend shopping list that starts at the top of the page; write 'm' for mummy. Write some or all of their name. Write some letters accurately.	Motivate children to write by providing opportunities in a wide range of ways. Suggestions: clipboards outdoors, chalks for paving stones, boards and notepads in the home corner. Children enjoy having a range of pencils, crayons, chalks and pens to choose from. Apps on tablets enable children to mix marks, photos and video to express meanings and tell their own stories. Children are also motivated by simple home-made books, different coloured paper and paper decorated with fancy frames. Help children to learn to form their letters accurately. First, they need a wide-ranging programme of physical skills development, inside and outdoors. Include large-muscle co-ordination: whole body, leg, arm and foot. This can be through climbing, swinging, messy play and parachute games etc. Plan for small-muscle co-ordination: hands and fingers. This can be through using scissors, learning to sew, eating with cutlery, using small brushes for painting and pencils for drawing. Children also need to know the language of direction ('up', 'down', 'round', 'back' etc).

Children in reception will be learning to:	Examples of how to support this:
Read individual letters by saying the sounds for them.	Help children to read the sounds speedily. This will make sound-blending easier.
Blend sounds into words, so that they can read short words made up of known letter—sound correspondences.	Ask children to work out the word you say in sounds: for example, h–a–t > hat; sh–o–p > shop. Show how to say sounds for the letters from left to right and blend them, for example, big, stamp.
Read some letter groups that each represent one sound and say sounds for them.	Help children to become familiar with letter groups, such as 'th', 'sh', 'ch', 'ee' 'or' 'igh'. Provide opportunities for children to read words containing familiar letter groups: 'that', 'shop', 'chin', 'feet', 'storm', 'night'. Listen to children read some longer words made up of letter-sound correspondences they know: 'rabbit', 'himself', 'jumping'.
Read a few common exception words matched to the school's phonic programme.	Note correspondences between letters and sounds that are unusual or that they have not yet been taught, such as 'do', 'said', 'were'.

Children in reception will be learning to:	Examples of how to support this:
Read simple phrases and sentences made up of words with known letter–sound correspondences and, where necessary, a few exception words.	Listen to children read aloud, ensuring books are consistent with their developing phonic knowledge. Do not include words that include letter-sound correspondences that children cannot yet read, or exception words that have not been taught. Children should not be required to use other strategies to work out words.
Re-read these books to build up their confidence in word reading, their fluency and their understanding and enjoyment.	Make the books available for children to share at school and at home. Avoid asking children to read books at home they cannot yet read.
Form lower-case and capital letters correctly.	Teach formation as they learn the sounds for each letter using a memorable phrase.
Spell words by identifying the sounds and then writing the sound with letter/s.	Show children how to touch each finger as they say each sound. For exception words such as 'the' and 'said', help children identify the sound that is tricky to spell.

Children in reception will be learning to:	Examples of how to support this:
Write short sentences with words with known sound–letter correspondences using a capital letter and full stop.	Support children to form the complete sentence before writing. Help children memorise the sentence before writing by saying it aloud. Only ask children to write sentences when they have sufficient knowledge of letter-sound correspondences.
Re-read what they have written to check that it makes sense.	Model how you read and re-read your own writing to check it makes sense.

Mathematics

Developing a strong grounding in number is essential so that all children develop the necessary building blocks to excel mathematically. Children should be able to count confidently, develop a deep understanding of the numbers to 10, the relationships between them and the patterns within those numbers. By providing frequent and varied opportunities to build and apply this understanding – such as using manipulatives, including small pebbles and tens frames for organising counting – children will develop a secure base of knowledge and vocabulary from which mastery of mathematics is built. In addition, it is important that the curriculum includes rich opportunities for children to develop their spatial reasoning skills across all areas of mathematics including shape, space and measures. It is important that children develop positive attitudes and interests in mathematics, look for patterns and relationships, spot connections, 'have a go', talk to adults and peers about what they notice and not be afraid to make mistakes.

Statutory framework for the early years foundation stage: early adopter version

Birth to three – babies, toddlers and young children will be learning to:	Examples of how to support this:
Combine objects like stacking blocks and cups. Put objects inside others and take them out again.	Encourage babies and young toddlers to play freely with a wide range of objects – toddlers engage spontaneously in mathematics during nearly half of every minute of free play. Suggestions: when appropriate, sensitively join in and comment on: • interestingly shaped objects like vegetables, wooden pegs, spoons, pans, corks, cones, balls • pots and pans, boxes and objects to put in them, shape sorters • stacking cups: hiding one, building them into a tower, nesting them and lining them up
Take part in finger rhymes with numbers. React to changes of amount in a group of up to three items.	Use available opportunities, including feeding and changing times for finger-play, outdoors and inside, such as 'Round and round the garden'. Sing finger rhymes which involve hiding and returning, like 'Two little dicky birds'.

Birth to three – babies, toddlers and young children will be learning to:	Examples of how to support this:
Compare amounts, saying 'lots', 'more' or 'same'. Counting-like behaviour, such as making sounds, pointing or saying some numbers in sequence.	Draw attention to changes in amounts, for example, by adding more bricks to a tower, or eating things up Offer repeated experiences with the counting sequence in meaningful and varied contexts, outside and indoors. Suggestions: count fingers and toes, stairs, toys, food items, sounds and actions.
Count in everyday contexts, sometimes skipping numbers – '1-2-3-5.'	Help children to match their counting words with objects. Suggestions: move a piece of apple to one side once they have counted it. If children are saying one number word for each object, it isn't always necessary to correct them if they skip a number. Learning to count accurately takes a long time and repeated experience. Confidence is important.
Climb and squeezing selves into different types of spaces. Build with a range of resources. Complete inset puzzles.	Describe children's climbing, tunnelling and hiding using spatial words like 'on top of', 'up', 'down' and 'through'. Provide blocks and boxes to play freely with and build with, indoors and outside. Provide inset puzzles and jigsaws at different levels of difficulty.

Birth to three – babies, toddlers and young children will be learning to:	Examples of how to support this:
Compare sizes, weights etc. using gesture and language – 'bigger/little/smaller', 'high/low', 'tall', 'heavy'.	Use the language of size and weight in everyday contexts. Provide objects with marked differences in size to play freely with. Suggestions: dolls' and adult chairs, tiny and big bears, shoes, cups and bowls, blocks and containers.
Notice patterns and arrange things in patterns.	Provide patterned material – gingham, polka dots, stripes etc. – and small objects to arrange in patterns. Use words like 'repeated' and 'the same' over and over.

3 & 4–year–olds will be learning to:	Examples of how to support this:
Fast recognition of up to 3 objects, without having to count them individually ('subitising'). Recite numbers past 5. Say one number for each item in order: 1,2,3,4,5. Know that the last number reached when counting a small set of objects tells you how many there are in total ('cardinal principle'). Show 'finger numbers' up to 5. Link numerals and amounts: for example, showing the right number of objects to match the numeral, up to 5.	Point to small groups of two or three objects: "Look, there are two!" Occasionally ask children how many there are in a small set of two or three. Regularly say the counting sequence, in a variety of playful contexts, inside and outdoors, forwards and backwards, sometimes going to high numbers. For example: hide and seek, rocket–launch count–downs. Count things and then repeat the last number. For example: "1, 2, 3 — 3 cars". Point out the number of things whenever possible; so, rather than just 'chairs', 'apples' or 'children', say 'two chairs', 'three apples', 'four children'. Ask children to get you a number of things, and emphasise the total number in your conversation with the child. Use small numbers to manage the learning environment. Suggestions: have a pot labelled '5 pencils' or a crate for '3 trucks'. Draw children's attention to these throughout the session and especially at tidy–up time: "How many pencils should be in this pot?" or "How many have we got?" etc.

3 & 4-year-olds will be learning to:	Examples of how to support this:
Experiment with their own symbols and marks as well as numerals. Solve real world mathematical problems with numbers up to 5. Compare quantities using language: 'more than', 'fewer than'.	Encourage children in their own ways of recording (for example) how many balls they managed to throw through the hoop. Provide numerals nearby for reference. Suggestions: wooden numerals in a basket or a number track on the fence. Discuss mathematical ideas throughout the day, inside and outdoors. Suggestions: • "I think Adam has got more crackers…" • support children to solve problems using fingers, objects and marks: "There are four of you, but there aren't enough chairs…." • draw children's attention to differences and changes in amounts, such as those in stories like 'The Enormous Turnip'.
Talk about and explore 2D and 3D shapes (for example, circles, rectangles, triangles and cuboids) using informal and mathematical language: 'sides', 'corners'; 'straight', 'flat', 'round'.	Encourage children to play freely with blocks, shapes, shape puzzles and shape-sorters. Sensitively support and discuss questions like: "What is the same and what is different?" Encourage children to talk informally about shape properties using words like 'sharp corner', 'pointy' or 'curvy'. Talk about shapes as you play with them: "We need a piece with a straight edge."

3 & 4-year-olds will be learning to:	Examples of how to support this:
Understand position through words alone — for example, "The bag is under the table," —with no pointing. Describe a familiar route. Discuss routes and locations, using words like 'in front of' and 'behind'.	Discuss position in real contexts. Suggestions: how to shift the leaves off a path, or sweep water away down the drain. Use spatial words in play, including 'in', 'on', 'under', 'up', 'down', 'besides' and 'between'. Suggestion: "Let's put the troll under the bridge and the billy goat beside the stream." Take children out to shops or the park: recall the route and the order of things seen on the way. Set up obstacle courses, interesting pathways and hiding places for children to play with freely. When appropriate, ask children to describe their route and give directions to each other. Provide complex train tracks, with loops and bridges, or water-flowing challenges with guttering that direct the flow to a water tray, for children to play freely with. Read stories about journeys, such as 'Rosie's Walk'.
Make comparisons between objects relating to size, length, weight and capacity.	Provide experiences of size changes. Suggestions: "Can you make a puddle larger?", "When you squeeze a sponge, does it stay small?", "What happens when you stretch dough, or elastic?" Talk with children about their everyday ways of comparing size, length, weight and capacity. Model more specific techniques, such as lining up ends of lengths and straightening ribbons, discussing accuracy: "Is it exactly…?"

3 & 4-year-olds will be learning to:	Examples of how to support this:
Select shapes appropriately: flat surfaces for building, a triangular prism for a roof etc.

Combine shapes to make new ones – an arch, a bigger triangle etc. | Provide a variety of construction materials like blocks and interlocking bricks. Provide den-making materials. Allow children to play freely with these materials, outdoors and inside. When appropriate, talk about the shapes and how their properties suit the purpose.

Provide shapes that combine to make other shapes, such as pattern blocks and interlocking shapes, for children to play freely with. When appropriate, discuss the different designs that children make. Occasionally suggest challenges, so that children build increasingly more complex constructions.

Use tidy-up time to match blocks to silhouettes or fit things in containers, describing and naming shapes. Suggestion: "Where does this triangular one /cylinder /cuboid go?"

 |

3 & 4-year-olds will be learning to:	Examples of how to support this:
Talk about and identifies the patterns around them. For example: stripes on clothes, designs on rugs and wallpaper. Use informal language like 'pointy', 'spotty', 'blobs' etc. Extend and create ABAB patterns — stick, leaf, stick, leaf. Notice and correct an error in a repeating pattern. Begin to describe a sequence of events, real or fictional, using words such as 'first', 'then...'	Provide patterns from different cultures, such as fabrics. Provide a range of natural and everyday objects and materials, as well as blocks and shapes, for children to play with freely and to make patterns with. When appropriate, children to continue patterns and spot mistakes. Engage children in following and inventing movement and music patterns, such as clap, clap, stamp. Talk about patterns of events, in cooking or getting dressed. Suggestions: • 'First', 'then', 'after', 'before' • "Every day we…" • "Every evening we…" Talk about the sequence of events in stories. Use vocabulary like 'morning', 'afternoon', 'evening' and 'night-time', 'earlier', 'later', 'too late', 'too soon', 'in a minute'. Count down to forthcoming events on the calendar in terms of number of days or sleeps. Refer to the days of the week, and the day before or day after, 'yesterday' and 'tomorrow'.

Children in reception will be learning to:	Examples of how to support this:
Count objects, actions and sounds.	Develop the key skills of counting objects including saying the numbers in order and matching one number name to each item.

Say how many there are after counting – for example, "...6, 7, 8. There are **8 balls**" – to help children appreciate that the last number of the count indicates the total number of the group. This is the cardinal counting principle.

Say how many there might be before you count to give a purpose to counting: "I think there are about 8. Shall we count to see?"

Count out a smaller number from a larger group: "Give me seven..." Knowing when to stop shows that children understand the cardinal principle.

Build counting into everyday routines such as register time, tidying up, lining up or counting out pieces of fruit at snack time.

Sing counting songs and number rhymes, and read stories that involve counting.

Play games which involve counting.

Identify children who have had less prior experience of counting, and provide additional opportunities for counting practice. |

Children in reception will be learning to:	Examples of how to support this:
Subitise.	Show small quantities in familiar patterns (for example, dice) and random arrangements. Play games which involve quickly revealing and hiding numbers of objects. Put objects into five frames and then ten frames to begin to familiarise children with the tens structure of the number system. Prompt children to subitise first when enumerating groups of up to 4 or 5 objects: "I don't think we need to count those. They are in a square shape so there must be 4." Count to check. Encourage children to show a number of fingers 'all at once', without counting.
Link the number symbol (numeral) with its cardinal number value.	Display numerals in order alongside dot quantities or tens frame arrangements. Play card games such as snap or matching pairs with cards where some have numerals and some have dot arrangements. Discuss the different ways children might record quantities (for example, scores in games), such as tallies, dots and using numeral cards.

Children in reception will be learning to:	Examples of how to support this:
Count beyond ten.	Count verbally beyond 20, pausing at each multiple of 10 to draw out the structure, for instance when playing hide and seek, or to time children getting ready. Provide images such as number tracks, calendars and hundred squares indoors and out, including painted on the ground, so children become familiar with two-digit numbers and can start to spot patterns within them.
Compare numbers.	Provide collections to compare, starting with a very different number of things. Include more small things and fewer large things, spread them out and bunch them up, to draw attention to the number not the size of things or the space they take up. Include groups where the number of items is the same. Use vocabulary: 'more than', 'less than', 'fewer', 'the same as', 'equal to'. Encourage children to use these words as well. Distribute items evenly, for example: "Put 3 in each bag," or give the same number of pieces of fruit to each child. Make deliberate mistakes to provoke discussion. Tell a story about a character distributing snacks unfairly and invite children to make sure everyone has the same.

Children in reception will be learning to:	Examples of how to support this:
Understand the 'one more than/one less than' relationship between consecutive numbers.	Make predictions about what the outcome will be in stories, rhymes and songs if one is added, or if one is taken away. Provide 'staircase' patterns which show that the next counting number includes the previous number plus one.
Explore the composition of numbers to 10.	Focus on composition of 2, 3, 4 and 5 before moving onto larger numbers Provide a range of visual models of numbers: for example, six as double three on dice, or the fingers on one hand and one more, or as four and two with ten frame images. Model conceptual subitising: "Well, there are three here and three here, so there must be six." Emphasise the parts within the whole: "There were 8 eggs in the incubator. Two have hatched and 6 haven't yet hatched." Plan games which involve partitioning and recombining sets. For example, throw 5 beanbags, aiming for a hoop. How many go in and how many don't?

Children in reception will be learning to:	Examples of how to support this:
Automatically recall number bonds for numbers 0–10.	Have a sustained focus on each number to 10. Make visual and practical displays in the classroom showing the different ways of making numbers to 10 so that children can refer to these. Play hiding games with a number of objects in a box, under a cloth, in a tent, in a cave, etc.: "Seven went in the tent and 2 came out. I wonder how many are still in there?" Intentionally give children the wrong number of things. For example: ask each child to plant 4 seeds then give them 1, 2 or 3. "I've only got 1 seed, I need 3 more." Spot and use opportunities for children to apply number bonds: "There are 6 of us but only 2 clipboards. How many more do we need?" Place objects into a five frame and talk about how many spaces are filled and unfilled. 

Children in reception will be learning to:	Examples of how to support this:
Select, rotate and manipulate shapes in order to develop spatial reasoning skills.	Provide high-quality pattern and building sets, including pattern blocks, tangrams, building blocks and magnetic construction tiles, as well as found materials. Challenge children to copy increasingly complex 2D pictures and patterns with these 3D resources, guided by knowledge of learning trajectories: "I bet you can't add an arch to that," or "Maybe tomorrow someone will build a staircase." Teach children to solve a range of jigsaws of increasing challenge.
Compose and decompose shapes so that children recognise a shape can have other shapes *within* it, just as numbers can.	Investigate how shapes can be combined to make new shapes: for example, two triangles can be put together to make a square. Encourage children to predict what shapes they will make when paper is folded. Wonder aloud how many different ways there are to make a hexagon with pattern blocks. Find 2D shapes within 3D shapes, including through printing or shadow play. 

Children in reception will be learning to:	Examples of how to support this:
Continue, copy and create repeating patterns.	Make patterns with varying rules (including AB, ABB and ABBC) and objects and invite children to continue the pattern. Make a deliberate mistake and discuss how to fix it.
Compare length, weight and capacity.	Model comparative language using 'than' and encourage children to use this vocabulary. For example: "This is heavier than that." Ask children to make and test predictions. "What if we pour the jugful into the teapot? Which holds more?"

Understanding the world

Understanding the world involves guiding children to make sense of their physical world and their community. The frequency and range of children's personal experiences increases their knowledge and sense of the world around them — from visiting parks, libraries and museums to meeting important members of society such as police officers, nurses and firefighters. In addition, listening to a broad selection of stories, non-fiction, rhymes and poems will foster their understanding of our culturally, socially, technologically and ecologically diverse world. As well as building important knowledge, this extends their familiarity with words that support understanding across domains. Enriching and widening children's vocabulary will support later reading comprehension.

Statutory framework for the early years foundation stage: early adopter version

Birth to three – babies, toddlers and young children will be learning to:	Examples of how to support this:
Repeat actions that have an effect. Explore materials with different properties. Explore natural materials, indoors and outside.	Encourage babies' explorations and movements, such as touching their fingers and toes. Show delight at their kicking and waving. Provide open-ended play materials inside and outdoors. Suggestion: Treasure Baskets for repeated exploration of textures, sounds, smells and tastes. Offer lots of different textures for exploration with fingers, feet and whole body. Suggestions: wet and dry sand, water, paint and playdough.
Explore and respond to different natural phenomena in their setting and on trips.	Encourage toddlers and young children to enjoy and explore the natural world. Suggestions: • standing in the rain with wellies and umbrellas • walking through tall grass • splashing in puddles • seeing the spring daffodils and cherry blossom • looking for worms and minibeasts • visiting the beach and exploring the sand, pebbles and paddling in the sea

Birth to three – babies, toddlers and young children will be learning to:	Examples of how to support this:
Explore and respond to different natural phenomena in their setting and on trips (continued).	Encourage children's exploration, curiosity, appreciation and respect for living things. Suggestions: • sharing the fascination of a child who finds woodlice teeming under an old log • modelling the careful handling of a worm and helping children return it to the dug-up soil • carefully planting, watering and looking after plants they have grown from seeds Encourage children to bring natural materials into the setting, such as leaves and conkers picked up from the pavement or park during autumn.
Make connections between the features of their family and other families.	Be open to children talking about differences and what they notice. For example, when children ask questions like: "Why do you wear a scarf around your head?" or "How come your hair feels different to mine?" Point out the similarities between different families, as well as discussing differences.

Birth to three – babies, toddlers and young children will be learning to:	Examples of how to support this:
Notice differences between people.	Model positive attitudes about the differences between people. Support children's acceptance of difference. Have resources which include: • positive images of people who are disabled • books and play materials that reflect the diversity of life in modern Britain • materials which confront gender stereotypes

3 & 4-year-olds will be learning to:	Examples of how to support this:
Use all their senses in hands-on exploration of natural materials. Explore collections of materials with similar and/or different properties. Talk about what they see, using a wide vocabulary.	Provide interesting natural environments for children to explore freely outdoors. Make collections of natural materials to investigate and talk about. Suggestions: • contrasting pieces of bark • different types of leaves and seeds • different types of rocks • different shells and pebbles from the beach Provide equipment to support these investigations. Suggestions: magnifying glasses or a tablet with a magnifying app. Encourage children to talk about what they see. Model observational and investigational skills. Ask out loud: "I wonder if…?" Plan and introduce new vocabulary, encouraging children to use it to discuss their findings and ideas.
Begin to make sense of their own life-story and family's history.	Spend time with children talking about photos, memories. Encourage children to retell what their parents told them about their life story and family.

3 & 4-year-olds will be learning to:	Examples of how to support this:
Show interest in different occupations.	Invite different people to visit from a range of occupations, such as a plumber, a farmer, a vet, a member of the emergency services or an author. Plan and introduce new vocabulary related to the occupation, and encourage children to use it in their talks and play.
Explore how things work	Provide mechanical equipment for children to play with and investigate. Suggestions: wind-up toys, pulleys, sets of cogs with pegs and boards.
Plant seeds and care for growing plants. Understand the key features of the life cycle of a plant and an animal. Begin to understand the need to respect and care for the natural environment and all living things.	Show and explain the concepts of growth, change and decay with natural materials. Suggestions: • plant seeds and bulbs so children observe growth and decay over time • observe an apple core going brown and mouldy over time • help children to care for animals and take part in first-hand scientific explorations of animal life cycles, such as caterpillars or chick eggs. Plan and introduce new vocabulary related to the exploration. Encourage children to use it in their discussions, as they care for living things. Encourage children to refer to books, wall displays and online resources. This will support their investigations and extend their knowledge and ways of thinking.

3 & 4-year-olds will be learning to:	Examples of how to support this:
Explore and talk about different forces they can feel.	Draw children's attention to forces. Suggestions: • how the water pushes up when they try to push a plastic boat under it • how they can stretch elastic, snap a twig, but can't bend a metal rod • magnetic attraction and repulsion Plan and introduce new vocabulary related to the exploration, and encourage children to use it.
Talk about the differences between materials and changes they notice.	Provide children with opportunities to change materials from one state to another. Suggestions: • cooking – combining different ingredients, and then cooling or heating (cooking) them • melting – leave ice cubes out in the sun, see what happens when you shake salt onto them Explore how different materials sink and float. Explore how you can shine light through some materials, but not others. Investigate shadows. Plan and introduce new vocabulary related to the exploration, and encourage children to use it.

3 & 4-year-olds will be learning to:	Examples of how to support this:
Continue to develop positive attitudes about the differences between people.	Ensure that resources reflect the diversity of life in modern Britain. Encourage children to talk about the differences they notice between people, whilst also drawing their attention to similarities between different families and communities. Answer their questions and encourage discussion. Suggestion: talk positively about different appearances, skin colours and hair types. Celebrate and value cultural, religious and community events and experiences. Help children to learn each other's names, modelling correct pronunciation.
Know that there are different countries in the world and talk about the differences they have experienced or seen in photos.	Practitioners can create books and displays about children's families around the world, or holidays they have been on. Encourage children to talk about each other's families and ask questions. Use a diverse range of props, puppets, dolls and books to encourage children to notice and talk about similarities and differences.

Children in reception will be learning to:	Examples of how to support this:
Talk about members of their immediate family and community.	During dedicated talk time, listen to what children say about their family. Share information about your own family, giving children time to ask questions or make comments. Encourage children to share pictures of their family and listen to what they say about the pictures. Using examples from real life and from books, show children how there are many different families.
Name and describe people who are familiar to them.	Talk about people that the children may have come across within their community, such as the police, the fire service, doctors and teachers. Listen to what children say about their own experiences with people who are familiar to them.
Comment on images of familiar situations in the past.	Present children with pictures, stories, artefacts and accounts from the past, explaining similarities and differences. Offer hands-on experiences that deepen children's understanding, such as visiting a local area that has historical importance. Show images of familiar situations in the past, such as homes, schools, and transport.

Children in reception will be learning to:	Examples of how to support this:
Comment on images of familiar situations in the past (continued).	Look for opportunities to observe children talking about experiences that are familiar to them and how these may have differed in the past. Offer opportunities for children to begin to organise events using basic chronology, recognising that things happened before they were born.
Compare and contrast characters from stories, including figures from the past.	Frequently share texts, images, and tell oral stories that help children begin to develop an understanding of the past and present. Feature fictional and non-fictional characters from a range of cultures and times in storytelling, listen to what children say about them. Draw out common themes from stories, such as bravery, difficult choices and kindness, and talk about children's experiences with these themes. In addition to storytelling, introduce characters, including those from the past using songs, poems, puppets, role play and other storytelling methods.

Children in reception will be learning to:	Examples of how to support this:
Draw information from a simple map.	Draw children's attention to the immediate environment, introducing and modelling new vocabulary where appropriate. Familiarise children with the name of the road, and or village/town/city the school is located in. Look at aerial views of the school setting, encouraging children to comment on what they notice, recognising buildings, open space, roads and other simple features. Offer opportunities for children to choose to draw simple maps of their immediate environment, or maps from imaginary story settings they are familiar with.
Understand that some places are special to members of their community.	Name and explain the purpose of places of worship and places of local importance to the community to children, drawing on their own experiences where possible. Take children to places of worship and places of local importance to the community. Invite visitors from different religious and cultural communities into the classroom to share their experiences with children.

Children in reception will be learning to:	Examples of how to support this:
Recognise that people have different beliefs and celebrate special times in different ways.	Weave opportunities for children to engage with religious and cultural communities and their practices throughout the curriculum at appropriate times of the year. Help children may begin to build a rich bank of vocabulary with which to describe their own lives and the lives of others.
Recognise some similarities and differences between life in this country and life in other countries.	Teach children about places in the world that contrast with locations they know well. Use relevant, specific vocabulary to describe contrasting locations. Use images, video clips, shared texts and other resources to bring the wider world into the classroom, listen to what children say about what they see. Avoid stereotyping and explain how children's lives in other countries may be similar or different in terms of how they travel to school, what they eat, where they live, and so on.

Children in reception will be learning to:	Examples of how to support this:
Explore the natural world around them.	Provide children with have frequent opportunities for outdoor play and exploration. Encourage interactions with the outdoors to foster curiosity and give children freedom to touch, smell and hear the natural world around them during hands-on experiences. Create opportunities to discuss how we care for the natural world around us. Offer opportunities to sing songs and join in with rhymes and poems about the natural world. After close observation, draw pictures of the natural world, including animals and plants. Observe and interact with natural processes, such as ice melting, a sound causing a vibration, light travelling through transparent material, an object casting a shadow, a magnet attracting an object and a boat floating on water.

Children in reception will be learning to:	Examples of how to support this:
Describe what they see, hear and feel whilst outside.	Encourage focused observation of the natural world. Listen to children describing and commenting on things they have seen whilst outside, including plants and animals. Encourage positive interaction with the outside world, offering children a chance to take supported risks, appropriate to themselves and the environment within which they are in. Name and describe some plants and animals children are likely to see, encouraging children to recognise familiar plants and animals whilst outside.
Recognise some environments that are different to the one in which they live.	Teach children about a range of contrasting environments within both their local or national region. Model the vocabulary needed to name specific features of the natural world, both natural and man-made. Share non-fiction texts that offer an insight into contrasting environments. Listen to how children communicate their understanding of their own environment and contrasting environments through conversation and in play.

Children in reception will be learning to:	Examples of how to support this:
Understand the effect of changing seasons on the natural world around them.	Guide children's understanding by draw children's attention to the weather and seasonal features. Provide opportunities for children to note and record the weather. Select texts to share with the children about the changing seasons. Throughout the year, take children outside to observe the natural world and encourage children to observe how animals behave differently as the seasons change. Look for children incorporating their understanding of the seasons and weather in their play.

Expressive arts and design

The development of children's artistic and cultural awareness supports their imagination and creativity. It is important that children have regular opportunities to engage with the arts, enabling them to explore and play with a wide range of media and materials. The quality and variety of what children see, hear and participate in is crucial for developing their understanding, self-expression, vocabulary and ability to communicate through the arts. The frequency, repetition and depth of their experiences are fundamental to their progress in interpreting and appreciating what they hear, respond to and observe.

Statutory framework for the early years foundation stage: early adopter version

Birth to three – babies, toddlers and young children will be learning to:	Examples of how to support this:
Show attention to sounds and music. Respond emotionally and physically to music when it changes. Move and dance to music. Anticipate phrases and actions in rhymes and songs, like 'Peepo'. Explore their voices and enjoy making sounds.	Babies are born ready to enjoy and make music from birth. Stimulate their enjoyment of music through singing and playing musical and singing games which are attuned to the baby. Provide babies, toddlers and young children with a range of different types of singing, sounds and music from diverse cultures. Music and singing can be live as well as pre-recorded. Play and perform music with different: • dynamics (loud/quiet) • tempo (fast/slow) • pitch (high/low) • rhythms (pattern of sound)
Join in with songs and rhymes, making some sounds. Make rhythmical and repetitive sounds. Explore a range of sound-makers and instruments and play them in different ways.	Introduce children to songs, including songs to go with routines. Suggestion: when washing hands, sing "This is the ways we wash our hands…". Provide children with instruments and with 'found objects'. Suggestions: tapping a bottle onto the table or running a twig along a fence. Encourage children to experiment with different ways of playing instruments.

Birth to three – babies, toddlers and young children will be learning to:	Examples of how to support this:
Notice patterns with strong contrasts and be attracted by patterns resembling the human face. Start to make marks intentionally. Explore paint, using fingers and other parts of their bodies as well as brushes and other tools. Express ideas and feelings through making marks, and sometimes give a meaning to the marks they make.	Ensure that the physical environment includes objects and materials with different patterns, colours, tones and textures for babies and young children to explore. Stimulate babies' and toddlers' early interest in making marks. Offer a wide range different materials and encourage children to make marks in different ways. Suggestions: • their fingers in cornflour • a stick in the mud • hands and feet in paint on different surfaces • tablets or computers Introduce colour names
Enjoy and take part in action songs, such as 'Twinkle, Twinkle Little Star'.	Introduce children to a broad selection of action songs from different cultures and languages. Sing songs regularly so that children learn the words, melody and actions off by heart. Encourage children to accompany action songs. They can do this with their own movements or by playing instruments.

Birth to three – babies, toddlers and young children will be learning to:	Examples of how to support this:
Start to develop pretend play, pretending that one object represents another. For example, a child holds a wooden block to her ear and pretends it's a phone.	Children generally start to understand the difference between pretend and real from around the age of 2. Help children to develop their pretend play by modelling, sensitively joining in and helping them to elaborate it. Suggestion: help to develop a child's home-corner play of feeding a 'baby', by suggesting a nappy-change and then a song as you settle the 'baby' to sleep.
Explore different materials, using all their senses to investigate them. Manipulate and play with different materials. Use their imagination as they consider what they can do with different materials. Make simple models which express their ideas.	Stimulate young children's interest in modelling. Suggestions: provide a wide range of found materials ('junk') as well as blocks, clay, soft wood, card, off-cuts of fabrics and materials with different textures. Provide appropriate tools and joining methods for the materials offered. Encourage young children to explore materials/ resources finding out what they are/what they can do, and decide how the they want to use them

3 & 4-year-olds will be learning to:	Examples of how to support this:
Take part in simple pretend play, using an object to represent something else even though they are not similar. Begin to develop complex stories using small world equipment like animal sets, dolls and dolls houses etc. Make imaginative and complex 'small worlds' with blocks and construction kits, such as a city with different buildings and a park.	Children generally start to develop pretend play with 'rules' when they 3 or 4 years old. Suggestion: offer pinecones in the home corner for children to pour into pans and stir like pasta. Some rules are self-created (the pole is now a horse, or the pinecones are now pasta in the pot). Other rules are group-created (to play in the home corner, you must accept the rule that one of your friends is pretending to be a baby). Provide lots of flexible and open-ended resources for children's imaginative play. Help children to negotiate roles in play and sort out conflicts. Notice children who are not taking part in pretend play, and help them to join in.

3 & 4-year-olds will be learning to:	Examples of how to support this:
Explore different materials freely, in order to develop their ideas about how to use them and what to make. Develop their own ideas and then decide which materials to use to express them. Join different materials and explore different textures.	Offer opportunities to explore scale. Suggestions: • long strips of wallpaper • child size boxes • different surfaces to work on e.g. paving, floor, tabletop or easel Listen and understand what children want to create before offering suggestions. Invite artists, musicians and craftspeople into the setting, to widen the range of ideas which children can draw on. Suggestions: glue and masking tape for sticking pieces of scrap materials onto old cardboard boxes, hammers and nails, glue guns, paperclips and fasteners.
Create closed shapes with continuous lines, and begin to use these shapes to represent objects. Draw with increasing complexity and detail, such as representing a face with a circle and including details. Use drawing to represent ideas like movement or loud noises.	Help children to develop their drawing and model-making. Encourage them to develop their own creative ideas. Spend sustained time alongside them. Show interest in the meanings children give to their drawings and models. Talk together about these meanings. Encourage children to draw from their imagination and observation.

3 & 4-year-olds will be learning to:	Examples of how to support this:
Show different emotions in their drawings and paintings, like happiness, sadness, fear etc. Explore colour and colour-mixing. Show different emotions in their drawings – happiness, sadness, fear etc.	Help children to add details to their drawings by selecting interesting objects to draw, and by pointing out key features to children and discussing them. Talk to children about the differences between colours. Help them to explore and refine their colour-mixing – for example: "How does blue become green?" Introduce children to the work of artists from across times and cultures. Help them to notice where features of artists' work overlap with the children's, for example in details, colour, movement or line.
Listen with increased attention to sounds. Respond to what they have heard, expressing their thoughts and feelings.	Help children to develop their listening skills through a range of active listening activities. Notice 'how' children listen well, for example: listening whilst painting or drawing, or whilst moving. Play, share and perform a wide variety of music and songs from different cultures and historical periods. Play sound-matching games.
Remember and sing entire songs. Sing the pitch of a tone sung by another person ('pitch match').	When teaching songs to children be aware of your own pitch (high/low). Children's voices are higher than adult voices. When supporting children to develop their singing voice use a limited pitch range. For example, 'Rain rain' uses a smaller pitch (high/low) range than many traditional nursery rhymes. Children's singing voices and their ability to control them is developing.

3 & 4-year-olds will be learning to:	Examples of how to support this:
Sing the melodic shape (moving melody, such as up and down, down and up) of familiar songs. Create their own songs, or improvise a song around one they know.	Encourage them to use their 'singing' voice: when asked to sing loudly, children often shout. Sing slowly, so that children clearly hear the words and the melody of the song. Use songs with and without words — children may pitch-match more easily without words. Try using one-syllable sounds such as 'ba'. Clap or tap to the pulse of songs or music, and encourage children to do this.
Play instruments with increasing control to express their feelings and ideas.	Offer children a wide range of different instruments, from a range of cultures. This might also include electronic keyboards and musical apps on tablets. Encourage children to experiment with different ways of playing instruments. Listen carefully to their music making and value it. Suggestion: record children's pieces, play the pieces back to the children and include them in your repertoire of music played in the setting.

Children in reception will be learning to:	Examples of how to support this:
Explore, use and refine a variety of artistic effects to express their ideas and feelings. Return to and build on their previous learning, refining ideas and developing their ability to represent them. Create collaboratively sharing ideas, resources and skills.	Teach children to develop their colour-mixing techniques to enable them to match the colours they see and want to represent, with step-by-step guidance when appropriate. Provide opportunities to work together to develop and realise creative ideas. Provide children with a range of materials for children to construct with. Encourage them to think about and discuss what they want to make. Discuss problems and how they might be solved as they arise. Reflect with children on how they have achieved their aims. Teach children different techniques for joining materials, such as how to use adhesive tape and different sorts of glue. Provide a range of materials and tools and teach children to use them with care and precision. Promote independence, taking care not to introduce too many new things at once. Encourage children to notice features in the natural world. Help them to define colours, shapes, texture and smells in their own words. Discuss children's responses to what they see. Visit galleries and museums to generate inspiration and conversation about art and artists.

Children in reception will be learning to:	Examples of how to support this:
Listen attentively, move to and talk about music, expressing their feelings and responses.	Give children an insight into new musical worlds. Introduce them to different kinds of music from across the globe, including traditional and folk music from Britain. Invite musicians in to play music to children and talk about it. Encourage children to listen attentively to music. Discuss changes and patterns as a piece of music develops.
Watch and talk about dance and performance art, expressing their feelings and responses.	Offer opportunities for children to go to a live performance, such as a pantomime, play, music or dance performance. Provide related costumes and props for children to incorporate into their pretend play.
Sing in a group or on their own, increasingly matching the pitch and following the melody.	Play pitch-matching games, humming or singing short phrases for children to copy. Use songs with and without words – children may pitch match more easily with sounds like 'ba'. Sing call-and-response songs, so that children can echo phrases of songs you sing. Introduce new songs gradually and repeat them regularly. Sing slowly, so that children can listen to the words and the melody of the song.

Children in reception will be learning to:	Examples of how to support this:
Develop storylines in their pretend play.	Provide a wide range of props for play which encourage imagination. Suggestions: different lengths and styles of fabric can become capes, the roof of a small den, a picnic rug or an invisibility cloak. Support children in deciding which role they might want to play and learning how to negotiate, be patient and solve conflicts. Help children who find it difficult to join in pretend play. Stay next to them and comment on the play. Model joining in. Discuss how they might get involved.
Explore and engage in music making and dance, performing solo or in groups.	Notice and encourage children to keep a steady beat, this may be whilst singing and tapping their knees, dancing to music, or making their own music with instruments and sound makers. Play movement and listening games that use different sounds for different movements. Suggestions: march to the sound of the drum or creep to the sound of the maraca. Model how to tap rhythms to accompany words, such as tapping the syllables of names, objects, animals and the lyrics of a song. Play music with a pulse for children to move in time with and encourage them to respond to changes: they could jump when the music suddenly becomes louder, for example. Encourage children to create their own music.

Children in reception will be learning to:	Examples of how to support this:
Explore and engage in music making and dance, performing solo or in groups (continued).	Encourage children to replicate choreographed dances, such as pop songs and traditional dances from around the world. Encourage children to choreograph their own dance moves, using some of the steps and techniques they have learnt.

Illustrations and artwork by <u>julidosad.co.uk</u> © **2020**

Many thanks to

Dr Julian Grenier, lead of the East London Research School and headteacher of Sheringham Nursery School and Children's Centre, for his work in developing this guidance, alongside the early years organisations, practitioners and professionals who kindly contributed their advice and expertise.

ICAN for giving permission for some of their materials on Communication and Language to be used and replicated within this guidance.

Nicola Burke, author of Musical Development Matters (MDM) and Early Education for giving permission for material from MDM to be used and replicated within this guidance. MDM can be downloaded in full from Early Education: https://www.early-education.org.uk/musical-development-matters

Printed in Great Britain
by Amazon